KNOWING
GOD
THROUGH
PRAYER

JIM GEORGE

HARVEST HOUSE PUBLISHERS
EUGENE, OREGON

Cover by Dugan Design Group

Previously published as *The Remarkable Prayers of the Bible*

KNOWING GOD THROUGH PRAYER
Copyright © 2005 Jim George
Published by Harvest House Publishers
Eugene, Oregon 97402
www.harvesthousepublishers.com

ISBN 978-0-7369-7057-0 (pbk.)
ISBN 978-0-7369-7058-7 (eBook)

Library of Congress Cataloging-in-Publication Data
    George, Jim, 1943-
    The remarkable prayers of the Bible / Jim George.
        p. cm.
    ISBN-10: 0-7369-1544-3 (pbk.)
    ISBN-13: 978-0-7369-1544-1
    1. Bible—Prayers. I. Title.
    BS680.P64G46 2005
    242'.722—dc22
                                                    2005005012

Printed in the United States of America

16 17 18 19 20 21 22 23 24 / BP-CD / 10 9 8 7 6 5 4 3 2 1

Contents

A Word for the Journey

Have you ever thought about how privileged you are to be able to talk to the God of the universe in prayer? And, through the Bible, to listen in on the prayers of the men and women who followed God?

God's Word says, "Out of the abundance of the heart the mouth speaks" (Matthew 12:34), and the prayers recorded in the Bible offer us a glimpse into the hearts of those who uttered them, not out of a sterile vacuum, but in the midst of real life. From these down-to-earth people, we hear:

- Prayers of people who simply enjoyed talking to God.

- Prayers filled with joy, anguish, and every emotion in between.

- Prayers that give insight into the character and desires of those praying.

- Prayers uttered from human beings who were honest, in need, and vulnerable.

- Prayers that reveal the strengths and weaknesses of those communing with God.

- Prayers that expose these men and women as people—just like you and me—who wanted nothing more than to *know* God.

As you listen to the prayers of men and women in the Bible, you will have the opportunity to examine the content of their lives and witness their pattern of prayer. You will discover what was occurring in their lives that gave birth to their heartfelt communications with God. You will also learn about the noble qualities that were nurtured because of their devotion to spending time with their heavenly Father.

Your journey in knowing God through prayer will help you grow in your faith in God and your understanding of the importance of prayer. Each chapter includes valuable "Lessons to Learn about Prayer" and capsulized "Prayer Principles" you'll find helpful for your own communion with God. And finally, I have provided a sample prayer to stimulate your own quests in knowing God.

What will the outcome of reading this book be for you personally? I'm praying you will be...

encouraged to pray more regularly,
stimulated to know God better through prayer,
moved to intercede for others, and
challenged to become more of a person of powerful prayer.

My friend, what you will find in this book is information from the Bible—about real people and about prayer—that will transform your life. May God strengthen and bless you as you make the journey of your life—the journey to knowing God through prayer.

1

Prayers to God in Faith

*He believed in the L*ORD*, and [God]*
accounted it to him for righteousness.

—GENESIS 15:6

I have often heard that if you want to see the worst in people, go on a trip with them. Travel usually brings out a person's dark side, doesn't it? But not in everyone. Take my wife, Elizabeth, for example. Talk about a trooper! A dyed-in-the-wool homebody, Elizabeth's adventures all started in the middle of the night some 20 years ago. That's when I called her (collect, of course) from a pay phone at Changi Airport in Singapore, and asked her to start praying about doing missions work on that tiny dot of an island in the South China Sea.

Well, that was only the beginning! After much prayer and counsel, I uprooted Elizabeth and our two daughters, and off we went to Singapore...stopping in Taiwan for a week (and a typhoon!)...then two weeks in the Philippines in missionary guest housing...then on to Singapore for a year, living out of suitcases and relocating from place to place, never finding a place to call home...and finally, back to the United States...only to move four times before we could resettle into our former home. And our lives have been a little like that ever since.

Yes, travel can reveal the dark side of people. But, as in our case, it can also expose the best. I can't tell you how many times our faith in God and His plans for us were challenged during our many ministry travels through the decades. As we have learned to pray and trust God for His protection and His provision, our faith (especially during that year going to and back from Singapore) has definitely been tested...and strengthened.

The Testing of Faith

Some 4000 years ago, there was another man—and family—who experienced an even greater test of faith in almighty God. His name was Abraham, the father of the Jewish nation.

Just imagine hearing this directive: "Get out of your country, from your family...to a land that I will show you" (Genesis 12:1). With these words, God presented Abraham with a test of faith. He asked Abraham to pull up his tent stakes, leave his relatives, and go to a distant land—a land to be named later. Travel today is difficult and can be brutal, but imagine taking a trip 4000 years ago! At that time travel was a major undertaking. Very few people ever left the safety of their local town, let alone trekked out across hundreds of miles of desert.

When God sends a test, His children have choices to make. And the same was true for Abraham. He could have said, "No thank You, God. Not enough assurances. Too risky, Lord!"—but he didn't. He accepted the challenge. He "passed the test," so to speak. He responded in faith.

Faith in God became a signature mark of Abraham's life. From the beginning of his journey with God, whether he heard the Lord speak directly to him or in visions, Abraham listened, believed, trusted, and obeyed. Oh, he didn't always understand. Often he "talked" things over with God through prayer. And sometimes he tried to interject his own reasoning into his prayer discussions with God. But in the end, Abraham "believed God" (Genesis 15:6) and became a channel of blessing to the nations (12:3).

I'm sure you are like me and most of God's people who want to be a man or woman of great prayer and great faith. So in this chapter, let's travel alongside Abraham as he takes his journey of faith—as he walks with God. Maybe...just maybe...we, too, can have our faith strengthened as we spend time on the road with Abraham, listening in on his remarkable prayers to God and eavesdropping on God's talks with him throughout his life.

Prayer in the Life of Abraham

We know very little about Abram's background. (Abram was Abraham's name before God changed it to reflect His covenant with Abraham—Genesis 17:5.) We do, however, know that Abraham was a descendant of Shem, one of Noah's sons, and that he married Sarai (later renamed Sarah), his half-sister. By God's sovereign choice of Abraham, we are privileged to follow the life of a man who, for sure, had feet of clay, just like you and me. But Abraham was also a man who made prayer a vital and natural part of his relationship with God. Abraham's prayers, offered up to God under a variety of circumstances and at different times in his life, give us a special opportunity to learn from the growth process of this remarkable man of faith and his prayers.

Abraham answered God's call—The first recorded message from God to Abraham appears in Genesis 12:1. Abraham's father, Terah, had just died. In this initial instance of communication between God and Abraham, God did all the talking: "Get out of your country...to a land that I will show you," God commanded.

And what was Abraham's response? Although no vocalized answer is recorded, the Bible reports that "Abram departed as the LORD had spoken to him" (verse 4).

Now fast-forward some 35 years to another test of Abraham's obedience. Abraham had prayed and waited for a son for 25 years. And at last God had provided the promised heir (21:1-3). Well, it's one thing to be asked to leave your country, but this time God gave a very different kind of command: "Take now your son, your only son Isaac, whom you love...and offer him...as a burnt offering" (22:2).

What did Abraham do? (And what would you as a mother or father do?) Without a word, immediately and early the next morning, Abraham obeyed (verse 3). Talk about impressive faith and trust in God! Again Abraham demonstrated what the bottom-line response to God should always be—obedience. And, as you probably know from this ancient story, the Angel of the Lord intervened as Abraham stretched out his hand to sacrifice his son (22:11-12).

On both ends of Abraham's life his obedience was tested. And on both occasions, Abraham did not resist God's direction. He did not verbalize any objection. By his actions he was saying *yes* in his heart. There may have been a few doubts as he packed up and moved out into the unknown, but he moved out in obedience. There were probably many fears and questions in Abraham's heart as he and Isaac climbed the hill where he was to sacrifice his son. But without a word and without hesitation, Abraham was willing to obey.

A Lesson to Learn about Prayer

What are your daily actions saying about your heart attitude? Is your attitude one of obedience? What evidence is there of your unspoken yeses to God's communication to you by His Spirit, and through His Word? What answers from God are you resisting? Ask God to increase your faith as you step out into an unknown future. Ask Him to give you a heart willing to obey. May this be your prayer, "Speak, for your servant is listening" (1 Samuel 3:10 NIV).

Abraham prayed to God and worshiped—From the start of Abraham's journey with God and throughout his life, Abraham built altars as he moved through the land God promised to him. He offered sacrifices on these altars and prayed to God (Genesis 12:8 and 13:4). These altars of worship, set up in the midst of a pagan world, served as a public witness to Abraham's commitment to the one true God.

A Lesson to Learn about Prayer

Prayer testifies to our faith in God. Building an altar and praying were to Abraham what "giving a blessing" over our food in a busy restaurant represents for us today. Everyone sees you pray! By this one act you make a statement: "I owe my food to the providence and provision of God. I am one of His people, and I am acknowledging my dependence on Him, even down to the very food I eat." Have you built any altars lately? Have you publicly shown your devotion to God?

Abraham sometimes forgot to pray—There was a time in my life when I wasn't seeking God's guidance for anything. I had drifted far from God, and I knew it. Not only had I forgotten to pray, I didn't want to pray! And I refused to take any steps toward getting right with God. Naturally, during that time of failing to seek God's guidance, I made some wrong choices. So I can sure relate to Abraham during this next period of his life.

By faith, Abraham answered God's call and entered the land of God's promise, where he built an altar to the Lord. But something happened. A famine developed in the land. *What should I do?* he wondered. *I should go where there's food, right? That's just pure common sense!* This seems to be Abraham's reasoning, for he went off to Egypt during the famine in search of food.

It appears that Abraham reacted to his circumstances without praying for God's guidance. Whatever confidence and spiritual maturity Abraham had developed during his brief time in the land of Canaan, it seemed to evaporate as he entered Egypt. What happened when Abraham relied on himself rather than God? He failed on these three counts!

- Abraham feared for his life (12:12). He thought he would starve to death. Fear is a good indicator that we have strayed away from God's will, for when we have fear, we are not trusting God.

- Abraham lied about his wife. He asked Sarah to join with him in lying about their relationship, and to say she was his sister (verse 13). Rationalizing our actions to justify doing something wrong is another sign that we are acting out of the will of God.

- Abraham chose a coward's approach. He opted not to defend Sarah when she was taken into Pharaoh's palace (verse 15). Failure to stand up for what is right is yet another mark of erring behavior.

How different the story might have been if Abraham had asked God for the wisdom to know what to do! Maybe if he had talked to God about the famine, God would have reminded him of His promise to bless Abraham and make his name great (verses 2-3).

Scripture tells us, God protected Abraham and Sarah from the consequences of their fear, lies, and wrong choices. But what about you? What happens if you go off in a direction without consulting God? God may choose to intervene, or He may allow you to suffer the consequences of your actions. You and I must never presume God will bail us out of the messes we make or get into, especially if we elect to disobey Him.

A Lesson to Learn about Prayer

No issue or decision is too minor for prayer. Take nothing for granted when it comes to your concerns. What may have seemed like "no brainers" to Abraham (during a famine—go where the food is, right?...and when you're about to die, lie!) were his opportunities to trust God. Take nothing for granted when it comes to seeking God's guidance. No issue or problem should ever be seen as too small for seeking God's input. The next time you are considering something "obvious," something that seems to be so clear-cut as to not require prayer, think again... and quickly get down on your knees and cry out to God.

Abraham responded in faith—Prayer is how we communicate with God. And how does God communicate with us? Our prayers are answered as the Holy Spirit moves our heart when we read Scripture or as we experience events or circumstances, and also through the guidance of wise counselors. But Abraham didn't have the indwelling Spirit. And he didn't have the Bible. And there were no counselors. So Abraham went through life relying totally on his relationship with God.

But having only God was all Abraham needed! So through prayer he expressed his questions and concerns to God about His promises to give him a son. To Abraham, prayer was as natural as talking with a friend or counselor. And on many occasions God, like a friend or counselor, answered Abraham's prayers verbally. Here's how one such prayer session went.

After God gave Abraham a great victory in the rescue of his nephew Lot (see Genesis 14), Abraham refused the offer of wealth from the wicked king of Sodom. He insisted instead on trusting in "the LORD, God Most High, the Possessor of heaven and earth" (14:22). Then, in a vision, God said, "Do not be afraid, Abram. I am your shield, your exceedingly great reward" (15:1).

In response to this encouragement from God and His promise of reward, Abraham voiced what seems to be a complaint. It's possible Abraham was thinking, *What could possibly have any real reward to me, seeing I still have no son?* When he asked, "What will You give me, seeing I go childless, and the heir of my house is Eliezer of Damascus?" (verse 2).

Abraham continued the conversation, voicing what had been bothering him for years. "Look, You have given me no offspring; indeed one born in my house is my heir!" (verse 3). Unable to see how God would fulfill His promise, Abraham put forth Eliezer, his most trusted servant, as the potential heir. And God said, "No."

God then took this aged and sorrowing man outside and gave him this astounding visual promise: "Look now toward heaven, and count the stars if you are able to number them....so shall your descendants be" (verse 5). It was then Abraham responded with total trust—"he believed in the LORD, and He accounted it to him for righteousness" (verse 6).

In this prayer session with God, you and I can see how much Abraham had grown in his walk of faith. From a man who was fearful, hesitant, and uncertain about relying totally on God,

Abraham had been transformed. It wasn't an easy process. No, his fears for his life, his selfishness, his lack of faith all had to be dealt with. But slowly, his life was changed.

A Lesson to Learn about Prayer

Prayer is an act of faith. Prayer is talking to someone you can't see, about something you don't have, with no visible means of obtaining it. That's exactly what Abraham's life was all about—living a life of faith! He provides a wonderful lesson for you and me: Our trust at times may falter as it did with Abraham. But as the years go by and you see your prayers answered, as you taste more and more of God's goodness, your faith grows. Doubts and fears will fade, to be replaced by a steadfast confidence in God. You can most assuredly say along with King Solomon, "There has not failed one word of all His good promise" (1 Kings 8:56).

Abraham prayed for others—One of the greatest examples in the Bible of intercessory prayer appears in Genesis 18. On this occasion, God visited Abraham as the Angel of the Lord. God came to tell Abraham two things: First, He was going to fulfill His long-standing promise to Abraham of a son (18:10). And second, He was going to judge Sodom and Gomorrah for their wickedness (verses 20-21).

Abraham was extremely troubled by what God promised for Sodom and Gomorrah because his nephew Lot lived there. So he expressed his concern in a series of prayers, appealing to God's justice. "Would You also destroy the righteous with the wicked?" (verse 23).

After a back-and-forth negotiation with God ("Suppose there were fifty righteous within the city...forty-five...forty...thirty...twenty...ten"), Abraham won a promise from God. "I will not destroy it for the sake of ten" (verses 24-32). In the end, God, of course, did what was right. Unfortunately, there weren't even ten righteous men in either city. God saved Lot and his two daughters, and destroyed all the wicked people in the two cities.

A Lesson to Learn about Prayer

From this interaction between God and Abraham, we learn three lessons about prayer.

First, answers to our prayers are not always immediate. Abraham waited 25 years before God gave him a son. Could you wait 25 years for answers to your prayers? Could you be satisfied if one or all of your prayers were never answered to your satisfaction? We must come to God praying, "Your will be done" (Matthew 6:10), not ours.

Second, our prayers should be motivated by a desire to see God glorified. While Abraham was concerned about the fate of the people in the two cities, he was more concerned about God's character, asking, "Shall not the Judge of all the earth do right?" (Genesis 18:25).

Third, God's love for the lost is greater than ours. God did not reprimand Abraham for his interest in sinners. It was God Himself who said, "I have no pleasure in the death of the wicked" (Ezekiel 33:11). As God encouraged Abraham, so He encourages us to pray for those without Christ. Never stop beseeching God for lost family and friends.

Abraham made a wrong decision—With all his wonderful qualities and his remarkable prayer life, Abraham had his weaknesses, too. Ten years after God spoke forth His covenant to make Abraham the father of a great nation (Genesis 12:2), Abraham had a huge lapse in his trust in God's promise to provide an heir.

That's a long time to wait. And apparently Abraham forgot that God had reaffirmed His covenant in the intervening years (Genesis 15:1-7). Abraham also seemed to forget that when he had prayed for an assurance and asked, "LORD God, how shall I know...?" (verse 8), God staged an elaborate visual ceremony to affirm his promises to Abraham (verses 9-20).

But after all those years of waiting, Abraham faced the same serious problem—he still had no son. True, he had believed God when He reconfirmed His promise to give him a son through Sarah (verse 6). But, with each passing year, the promise seemed further and further from becoming a reality. Both he and his wife were not getting any younger. *How could God's promise be fulfilled?* he questioned.

While Abraham was thinking this problem through, Sarah made a suggestion that was common for the culture of that day: "Go in to my maid; perhaps I shall obtain children by her" (16:2). And to make the proposal even more acceptable, Sarah used God to justify it: "the LORD has restrained me from bearing children" (verse 2).

Somehow it never seemed to enter either Abraham or Sarah's minds to consult with God about this plan they were cooking up. If they had prayed, God might have refreshed their memories with these facts:

- Had He not protected Abraham and Sarah as they crossed the desert into the land of Caanan? Yes.

- Had He not rescued them from their blunder in Egypt when they lied to Pharaoh about their marital relationship? Yes.

- Had He not spoken directly to Abraham in the not-too-distant past and promised (again) that He would give them a son? A resounding *yes!*

You would think that the man who personally knew "the LORD, God Most High, the possessor of heaven and earth" (14:22) would have continued to trust Him to cause Sarah to bear a son. You would think that the man who had heard God promise to be his "shield" and "reward" (15:1) would have never faltered in faith. Even after his long history with God, Abraham did not consult God about his options. Thus, he made a wrong decision, which was based on three false assumptions:

- Abraham wrongfully assumed Sarah's arguments were valid. The fact that she brought God into her reasoning clouded Abraham's thinking.

- Abraham wrongfully assumed Sarah's solution would make her happy and content. It was the old "end justifies the means" reasoning. But as the scenario unfolded, Sarah's unhappiness produced further sadness as the pregnant servant came to despise Sarah, her mistress (16:4-6).

- Abraham wrongfully assumed the customs of the pagans surrounding him were acceptable. You don't have to read very far in the Bible to see God's ideal for marriage—one man for one woman (2:18-25)—quickly perverted (4:19). And here, Abraham goes against God's ideal. Without consulting God, he gave in to the social pressure of his day. (Does this sound familiar?)

What a disaster! Abraham was deceived by his own emotions and misled by his wife's less-than-pure motives. All he wanted was to do God's will. Even though he had the right motives, he went about the matter in the wrong way. He took things into his own hands and created a situation the world is still dealing with today—the ages-old turmoil between the Arabs (Ishmael, Abraham's son by Hagar) and the Jews (Isaac, Abraham's son by Sarah).

A Lesson to Learn about Prayer

What can help us make the right kinds of decisions as we seek to follow and do God's will? You and I should never assume on possible solutions in our situation. Seek wisdom from God and wise, godly counselors who can help you see all the options that are available. Then ask God to help you determine your best option—the one that will most glorify Him. Don't do what Abraham didn't do—don't fail to pray over your decisions. Prayer is the starting point for every decision you make.

The story of Abraham's growing faith should be a big encouragement to each of us. There were times when Abraham displayed very little faith. He had failures, and he compromised at difficult times in his life. Yet his responses show us that faith grows, not in the absence of struggle, but in the midst of it. Like Abraham, you and I will face setbacks and trials. The key to growing more mature in your faith and trust in God is to seek His wisdom. Pray and ask Him for direction. Then, when each trial comes (and come they will!), you can trust God to see you through.

Prayer Principles for You—Faith

Prayer guards you against taking matters into your own hands.

What is the first question you usually ask yourself when confronted with a decision? *What can I do?* This question looks at your capabilities. You may wonder, *Do I have the skills, money, power to make my decision a reality?* Or sometimes you may ask, *What should I do?* This deals with morality—doing what's right, fair, just.

When it's time to make a decision, the best question to ask is, "God, what do You want me to do?" This question shows a dependence on the Lord in any given situation. When it came to having a son, Abraham failed to pray and took matters into his own hands...and the world is still living with the disastrous results.

Prayer guards you against making quick decisions.

How often are you asked to make "spur of the moment" decisions? "We need an answer...right now!" is a statement we hear too often. And, in the heat of the moment and under the pressure of urgency, you might make a quick decision that requires months or even years to undo the consequences. Abraham made a bad decision and used his wife's maidservant to have a child. If a quick decision is needed and there's no time to pray about it, then the answer is *no!* No decision made without prayer!

Prayer guards you against being influenced by family and friends.

Sometimes it's hard to make good decisions based on the advice of close family members. You're just that—too close! Your relationship can color your judgment. And sometimes family members aren't as spiritually mature as they should be. Or they are so close to you and your problem that they cannot be objective. As a result, their advice is often tainted by emotion, sin, selfishness, or worldliness.

But when you pray, you're able to seek the mind of God rather than the mind of man. Sarah wanted a son, and came up with a humanistic and man-centered solution. Don't do what Abraham did—he listened to family instead of praying to God.

Prayer guards you against the influence of your culture.

To some extent, you are a product of your culture. Society has a powerful influence over everyone, and no one is immune to the world. Therefore it's possible for many of your decisions to be influenced by the standards set by your culture.

However, just because something is acceptable in society doesn't make it right. Prayer can keep you from looking at your decisions-to-be-made through culturally colored glasses...like Abraham did. Prayer forces you to ask, "God, what is Your standard? What does Your Word say I should do in this situation?"

Prayer guards you against missing God's will.

When you don't pray, your heart and emotions can dictate your direction and you can miss God's will. What does the Bible say about your heart? It is "deceitful above all things, and desperately wicked; who can know it?" (Jeremiah 17:9). To ensure that your feelings and desires don't hinder you from choosing God's will, make sure you pray. Pray until your heart and emotions are neutral. Then you can better "hear" God speak to you through His Word and through wise counsel.

A Prayer to Grow in Faith

God Almighty—El Shaddai! This is the name You used for Yourself when You promised Abraham he would have many descendants. Your name *El Shaddai* speaks of Your unlimited power to fulfill Your promises to Abraham...and to me today as Your child. May I find confidence in You, and in Your love in choosing me for salvation through Your Son, Jesus Christ. May I, with confidence, stand alongside Abraham of old, having faith to believe, no matter what is happening around me. I know that You, El Shaddai, Almighty God, are with me in all Your unlimited power, by my side, protecting me as You guide my every step along Your path for me. Amen.[1]

2

Prayers Grow in Humility

Now the man Moses was very humble,
more than all men who were on
the face of the earth.

—Numbers 12:3

When you think of humility and a humble person, who do you think of? Your pastor? A friend? A business associate? A parent? Well, if you had to think for a while, then you are beginning to get a picture of how hard it is to find much humility in our society today!

In my years of ministry experience, I have had the privilege of meeting many remarkable and godly people who are truly humble. But the person who immediately came to my mind when I posed the aforementioned question to myself is Daniel Anderson, president of Appalachian Bible College.

Why Dan Anderson? Maybe Dr. A's (as his students affectionately call him) humility is captured in the motto of this dynamic Christian college located in the small town of Bradley, nestled in the beautiful Appalachian mountains of southern West Virginia:

"Because life is for service."

Maybe, too, Dr. Anderson's humility is understood by the school's ministry focus, of which he is its foremost model:

"Seeking to nurture
humble but confident
servant leaders."

You or I might try to guess at the reasons for this man's servant attitude, but if you were to spend just a few minutes with him, you would immediately detect the source of Dan Anderson's humility. It comes from a close and abiding relationship with the greatest of all servant leaders, the Lord Jesus Christ.

So, if you ever want an up-close-and-personal look at a great Christian leader—one who is also a humble servant—just take I-64, I-77, or I-79 South, from anywhere north of the college, until you reach Exit 48. You can't miss Appalachian Bible College. It's the place with 300 humble male and female servant leaders who are just like their mentor, Dan Anderson.

The Most Humble Man Alive

The importance of humility in God's men and women springs from the fact that this trait is a part of God's character. In Psalm

113:4-6, God is represented as being "high above all nations, His glory above the heavens." Yet He "humbles Himself to behold the things that are in the heavens and in the earth." Amazingly, wherever the quality of humility is found in the Old Testament, whether in a man or woman, it is praised. And if you look a little further, you'll discover God's blessing is given to those who possess humility.

Take Moses, for instance. The Bible reports, "Now the man Moses was very humble, more than all men who were on the face of the earth" (Numbers 12:3). That's God's description of the man Moses, who was chosen by God—at age 80!—to lead His people out of Egypt. And yet, a look at Moses' first 80 years of life reveals a far different man than the one spoken of in Numbers 12:3. Humility wasn't always so evident in Moses' life.

Where did Moses' humility come from? And how was it developed? Answers emerge as we divide Moses' life into thirds, into three different phases.

Phase 1: From slave to prince—Every Sunday school child has heard the story of baby Moses. Born to parents who served Pharaoh in Egypt, little Moses was found by Pharaoh's daughter while he was floating on the Nile River in a basket. Moses was then adopted by this Egyptian princess. As her child, he was raised and educated in the palace of Pharaoh, the most powerful leader in the world at that time (Exodus 2:1-10).

Phase 2: From prince to shepherd—But at age 40, in the foolish act of trying to save a fellow Hebrew, Moses killed an Egyptian. On the next day, a further attempt to assist his people revealed that his act of murder the day before was known to others. To escape capture, he ran for his life. Moses' attempts at delivering his people in his own power had failed in a big way (verses 11-15).

So for the next one-third of his life, Moses enjoyed the quiet existence of an exile, living as a wilderness shepherd with a small group of Midianites. This was a far cry from life in the palace! During this second 40 years, Moses' dreams of delivering his people began to fade (Acts 7:25). His grand vision of his personal abilities began to shrink until, at last, he was ready for the task God had in mind for him all along. He was finally the humble servant God needed for the task of leading His people out of Egypt.

Phase 3: From shepherd to leader—The last 40 years of Moses' life were years of powerful, dynamic leadership and humble service. Moses was not like other leaders of his day—autocratic and prideful. No, his style was characterized by prayer and a humble dependence on God.

Chart this progression: At 40 years of age, Moses mistakenly "supposed that his brethren would have understood that God would deliver them by his hand" (Acts 7:25). By the time Moses was 80, God enjoyed a relationship with Moses unlike His relationships with others (at least during Moses' lifetime). Listen as God describes and defends this relationship in Numbers 12:6-8:

> 6 Hear now My words: If there is a prophet
> among you, I, the LORD, make Myself known
> to him in a vision; I speak to him in a dream.

7 Not so with My servant Moses; He is faithful
in all My house.
8 I speak with him face to face, even plainly,
and not in dark sayings; and he sees the form
of the LORD.

Moses' unique face-to-face interactions with God would empower
him to deliver God's people from the oppression of the Egyptians.
And over Moses' last 40 years, this prayer relationship would provide Moses with the strength, courage, wisdom, and humility he
needed to lead a very stubborn group of people to the borders of
the Promised Land.

Prayer in the Life of Moses

As we look now at the prayers and life of Moses, I can't help but
think of what James says regarding the prayers of godly men and
women:

> The effective, fervent prayer of a righteous
> man avails much (James 5:16).

Moses truly personified this truth. And his powerful habit of
intercession was more than a match for the constant murmuring
of the two million cantankerous people who were under his leadership for 40 years. What can we learn from Moses' prayer life?

Moses prayed expecting a response—Moses' first encounter
with God came while he was tending sheep near a mountain called
Horeb (Exodus 3:1). It was there Moses observed a burning bush
that "was not consumed" (verse 2). When he turned to take a

better look at this phenomenon, God began a conversation with Moses. (Later, in a matter of months, Moses would lead the two million complaining Israelites to Horeb, also called Sinai, the very mountain where he first talked with God. There, too, he and the people would receive the Ten Commandments from the hand of God—Exodus 19:11.)

Throughout this prayer encounter with God, Moses and God carried on an active conversation—"And the LORD said...And Moses said unto God..." (Exodus 3:1–4:17). Here we see that true prayer is ongoing, and that it is a two-way channel. We speak to God, and God speaks to us. For instance, when Moses questioned God about his lack of personal abilities and presented his list of excuses as to why he wasn't the right person for the job, God answered back to each of Moses' objections. This prayer reads like a dialogue in a play. It is full of life, with one speaker seeming to argue with the other. One questions, and the other answers.

Simply put, prayer is communication between two parties— between you and God. When you or I unburden our heart to God, we should expect Him to speak to us through His Word and/or the events in our lives. God may answer *yes*, *no*, or *wait*, but God will answer!

But perhaps, as with Moses, God's answer is one you or I don't want to hear. What if it's an answer not to our liking and we (like Moses) want to argue with God about it? We've received divine direction, but maybe we (like Moses) want to make excuses about why we can't or won't respond to God's will. And maybe (like Moses again) we want to shrink back while explaining to God why He can't use us, why we're the wrong person. That's exactly what Moses did. Listen in on his hesitancy...and learn a lesson!

- "Who am I that I should go?" (Exodus 3:11).

- "What shall I say to them?" (3:13).

- "But suppose they will not believe me or listen to my voice?" (4:1).

- "I am slow of speech" (4:10).

A Lesson to Learn about Prayer

Friend, what answers are you receiving from God that you don't like or want to hear? And what excuses are you making? You can refuse and, as with Moses, God may put an "Aaron" (Moses' brother) in your place (4:14-15). Don't miss out on God's blessing. God is speaking! He's giving you direction. Make sure you are listening and willing to accept His answers. He delights in talking to you and in answering your prayers. Make sure you delight in doing His will (Psalm 40:8).

Moses prayed prayers of praise—Sometimes we are so overjoyed by God's goodness that we break forth in praise. If prayer is simply communing with God, and praise is a way of voicing our thanks to Him, then prayer and praise go hand in hand. That's what happened with Moses on two occasions.

Moses' first outbreak of praise came early in the escape and exodus of God's people. Within a few days of leaving Egypt, things looked pretty bleak. Pharaoh had heard that the Israelites were wandering in the desert. His heart was hardened toward them, and he went after what he thought was a bewildered group lost in the desert (Exodus 14:3).

And there God's people were! One day they were on the verge of extinction, trapped by the sea before them and by Pharaoh's advancing army pursuing them from behind. But by the next morning, God had completely destroyed Pharaoh's forces, powerfully and miraculously drowning them in the sea (verses 5-31).

God's chosen people had every reason to rejoice—and rejoice they did! Hear now a part of the prayer of praise Moses and the people lifted to God Most High:

> I will sing to the LORD,
> for He has triumphed gloriously!
> The horse and its rider
> He has thrown into the sea!
> The LORD is my strength and song,
> and He has become my salvation;
> He is my God, and I will praise Him;
> My father's God, and I will exalt Him (15:1-2).

Moses' second song of prayer and praise came 40 years later on the plain of Moab. This outburst of praise was addressed to heaven as well as to earth (Deuteronomy 32:1). It was offered up in response to God's guidance and protection over the years. The words that formed this song were for the ears of God, as well as for the ears of the people (verse 44)…and today for your ears and mine:

> Give ear, O heavens, and I will speak;
> and hear, O earth, the words of my mouth…
> For I proclaim the name of the LORD:

Ascribe greatness to our God.
He is the Rock, His work is perfect;
for all His ways are justice,
a God of truth and without injustice;
righteous and upright is He (32:1-4).

A Lesson to Learn about Prayer

Our prayers should include praise and thanksgiving. Like Moses, we should have times when our prayer and praise are offered up audibly for all to hear. For we, like Moses and the Israelites, also have much to be thankful for. Moses said it well: "He is your praise, and He is your God, who has done these great and awesome things which your eyes have seen" (Deuteronomy 10:21). What are you thankful for right this minute?

Moses prayed prayers of intercession—Praying for others is a ministry and a responsibility. It seems Moses was constantly on his face before the Lord interceding and pleading for others. Note this handful of times when Moses mediated for others before God:

- Moses, at Pharaoh's urging, asked God to lift various plagues afflicting the Egyptians...and God responded (Exodus 8:8-11; 9:28-29; 10:17-19).

- Moses cried out to God in the wilderness to provide water and food for the people...and God provided (water—15:24-25; food—16:4).

- Moses held his staff up until sunset and interceded in prayer while Israel battled a band of Amalekites…and God brought victory (17:8-16).

- Moses pleaded twice with God not to destroy the people after they committed idolatry with a golden calf…and God spared them (32:9-14,30-34).

- Moses prayed for the people when God sent "fiery serpents" as a result of their complaints against both God and Moses… and God saved them (Numbers 21:5-9).

A Lesson to Learn about Prayer

In our day of selfish indulgence, it's refreshing to see God's servant humbly making requests not for himself, but for others. God pays attention to our prayers on behalf of others. He is merciful and hears the prayers of the righteous (Proverbs 15:29). Just as God listened to the prayers of one man—Moses—and thousands were blessed and protected, so God listens to your prayers. Only eternity will reveal the many (I hope and pray) who were blessed by your intercession! As one person said, "Prayer is the slender nerve that moves the muscles of Omnipotence."[2] Who needs your prayers today?

Moses prayed to God instead of complaining to others—Once Moses received his commission from God to lead the people, he brought his burdens and problems to God. He continually took his issues with Pharaoh to the Lord. And in every case, God gave him answers. Then in the wilderness, on the many occasions when the people disobeyed, Moses sought no other solace than that which God offered. He repeatedly came before the Lord and asked for strength to properly lead God's people.

A Lesson to Learn about Prayer

We are often tempted to tell our best friends—or anyone who will listen—about how badly others are treating us, about how awful things are. We take our problems to others who, more often than not, can't or won't do anything about them. Don't choose to bare your complaints to other people. Choose rather to take your problems to God—who can definitely do something about them! Do you have a matter you need to talk over with the Lord right now?

*Moses prayed for others regardless of how they treated him—*Jesus said to "pray for those who spitefully use you and persecute you" (Matthew 5:44). That seems to have been Moses' attitude as he spent 40 years praying for people who misinterpreted his motives, questioned his authority, were jealous of his leadership and his relationship with God, and made his life miserable. No matter what Moses did, someone had a problem with Moses and with his leadership! What did Moses do about it? He prayed.

- Moses prayed for those who *complained* against him because they had no food (Exodus 16:2-3).

- Moses prayed for those who *contended* with him because they had no water (17:1).

- Moses prayed for Aaron and Miriam after they *spoke out* against his leadership (Numbers 12:1-16).

- Moses prayed for the people who, out of fear, *refused* to enter the Promised Land (Numbers 16:5).

A Lesson to Learn about Prayer

Praying for our enemies and those who mean to do us harm is usually not our normal response, is it? This is where Moses' example of prayer and humility is vitally important. A truly humble man or woman would be more concerned for God's glory and for the person who means them ill than for themselves. What should our prayer response be for those who persecute us? Follow Jesus' example and pray, "Father, forgive them, for they do not know what they do" (Luke 23:34). Are there any "enemies" you need to pray for, to forgive?

Moses prayed for sinners—While Moses was on the mountain receiving the Ten Commandments, God informed him that the people were engaging in some terrible sins. Isolated from the awful scenes of sin, Moses retained his perspective and pleaded with God on behalf of the people. He told them, "You have committed a great sin. So now I will go up to the LORD; perhaps I can make atonement for your sin" (Exodus 32:30).

Then, in an inconceivable act of sacrificial devotion, Moses prayed to God, "Oh, these people have committed a great sin.... Yet now, if You will forgive their sin—but if not, I pray, blot me out of Your book which You have written" (verses 31-32).

A Lesson to Learn about Prayer

How burdened are you for those around you who are in sin? Do you have family and friends who say they are Christians but who are not walking with the Lord? Don't look the other way. And don't pretend it isn't happening. Show the same heartfelt compassion Moses showed. Follow the advice given in James 5:19-20: "Brethren, if anyone among you wanders from the truth, and someone turns him back, let him know that he who turns a sinner from the error of his way will save a soul from death and cover a multitude of sins." How faithful are you at praying for erring brothers and sisters?

Think with me again about the president of the Christian college I spoke of earlier. Recall the school's focus—"Seeking to nurture humble but confident servant leaders." Is this what you desire for your own life? Then, like God's remarkable servant Moses, and all who possess a degree of humility, you must nurture a close walk with God through prayer, for humility's strength is grounded in God.

Prayer Principles for You—Humility

Prayer reviews your motives.

Time spent in prayer enables you to put everything on pause and review your motivation. It gives you an opportunity to ask God, "Why am I doing this? Is it out of pride, selfishness, guilt, greed, fear...or out of love for You and others?" Moses had the right motives when he wanted to help his suffering brothers. But his motivation drove him to violate God's moral law. To do things God's way you must pause, pray, appraise your motives, and ask Him to show you the right way to proceed.

Prayer refines your methods.

As you take time to ask God for wisdom and guidance, He will lead you into His will for your life. God will also give you instructions about the methods you should use to accomplish His will. God promises to "instruct you and teach you in the way you should go" (Psalm 32:8). Like Moses in his zeal to help his brethren, your methods can be completely wrong. That's why prayer is important—it can help refine your methods as you ask, "Lord, how would *You* have me do this?"

Prayer restrains your emotions.

The next time your nerves are wearing thin or patience is in short supply, pray. Stop and ask God to calm your emotions, to clear your head, and to give you His self-control. If you are angry or hurt or in a hurry, pray for God to quiet your heart and restrain your emotions so you can act in a God-honoring way. Twice Moses' feelings got the best of him, and both times there were severe consequences. Remember, the wise person prays and obeys, while the fool sins and suffers.

Prayer revisits your options.

There are times when, like the children of Israel or like Moses, you can only see *one* option or solution. Yet there is always another alternative—God's solution! Through prayer you can ask God to give you a better—no, the best!—option. Prayer allows you time to think and talk through the issues and alternatives with your heavenly Father, to be spiritual in your decisions instead of fleshly, to be wise instead of foolhardy, to be godly instead of worldly.

Prayer regulates your timing.

All time around the globe is regulated by Greenwich Mean Time. And in a similar sense, your time and service to God are no different. They are regulated by God's perfect timing. So often we get in a panic to do things, to be of use, to get ahead, to move out, to be promoted. We become impatient and want to taste success—right now! That's what happened to Moses. God wanted to use Moses, but it would take 40 more years for God to mature him for the task. God wants to use you too, and He will regulate the timing for the events in your life. Your job in the meantime? Take care of the depth of your prayer life. Prayer will help you adjust your timing to God's plan and help you to mature while you wait.

Prayer recounts your resources.

God promises He has given you everything that pertains to life and godliness (2 Peter 1:3). This means that even when things look hopeless and you are in your darkest hour, you have all of God's rich resources at hand. Coming to the Lord in prayer and thanksgiving helps you to remember all He has already provided and promises to continue to provide.

There's no need to panic in times of desperation. Pray instead, and experience God's peace and provision for your every need. Recount His resources. They are there! Give humble thanks now for these few—life in Christ, the guidance of the Holy Spirit, mature Christians who can give you wise counsel, the power of prayer—and then add more to the list. You are blessed above all people! One day, like Moses, you will look back over a lifetime of God's provision. Moses was able to give thanks to God for 120 years of His mercies and faithfulness (Deuteronomy 7:9), and someday, you will be able to look back and thank God for all His goodness in your life.

A Prayer to Grow in Humility

Father, I am moved by the example of humility found in the life and prayers of Moses. Your Word tells me that Moses did not trust in his own abilities, but "ascribed greatness" to You, his God—"the Rock." What a vivid picture of Your power and stability! I believe that, in the same way that You were true to Your covenant with Israel, You, as my Rock, will never fail in Your promises to me. In the times that I falter, You are my unchanging and immovable Rock—my "chosen" stone, my "cornerstone," who will always be my security and safety. I am comforted to know that I can run to the Rock who is higher than I. I praise You that in You I will never be disappointed. Amen.[3]

3

Prayers to Grow in Gratitude

Hannah prayed and said:
My heart rejoices in the LORD;
My horn is exalted in the LORD.
—1 SAMUEL 2:1

Have you ever been in a spot where you asked yourself, "What am I doing here? Why did I choose this particular decision or direction?" One similar moment of questioning came to me some years back as I sat in a crowded train car on its way from Madras, India, to Bangalore, another city in India. This was my first trip to the country, which would have been stressful enough. But on this, my inaugural visit, I was alone, traveling to a city of five million people where I knew no one, having no idea where I would stay, and looking for a local Christian ministry with no address.

Even though I was beginning to question my sanity, I had boarded the train with full confidence that God was going to answer all my questions and provide for all my needs. Why? Well, for one, a group of my traveling companions had prayed together with me right before my train departed. They had asked God to give me a place to stay and to lead me to the ministry in question so I could give them a gift of money from our church family to buy Bibles for the people of that region. So off I went—a little apprehensive, but convinced that God would answer our prayers.

As I bounced back and forth on the hard wooden train bench and tried to read my Bible and calm my heart, a man came over and sat next to me. Excusing himself, he shyly explained, "I saw you reading your Bible from the other side of the train. I am a Christian living in Bangalore. If you don't have a place to stay tonight, my family and I would be honored for you to stay with us. And by the way, if you need to find any Christian ministries in the city, I am well aware of them all."

The answers to our group's prayers came within one hour of leaving Madras! You can imagine how grateful I was to Mr. Abraham Thomas for his hospitality and familiarity with the Christian community in Bangalore. And even more, how grateful I was to God!

Gratitude Should Characterize a Christian's Life

We become Christians by God's grace, through His unmerited favor. We can't buy salvation. We can't earn eternal life. All that

God offers in a relationship with Him through His Son Jesus Christ comes to us as a free gift. We have all that we need for life and godliness (2 Peter 1:3). And what's also amazing is that God hears and answers our prayers! With all that God has given us, we are truly blessed people! And we should sing praise along with the psalmist who declared, "It is good to give thanks to the LORD, and to sing praises to Your name, O Most High; to declare Your lovingkindness in the morning, and Your faithfulness every night" (Psalm 92:1-2).

On that train to Bangalore, I was very grateful to God for His answer to prayer and to Mr. Thomas for his kindness. And there are *many* more things you and I can thank God for. Thankfulness should characterize every aspect of our life. "Thank You, Lord" should be recurring words throughout our day.

There is a woman in the Bible who shows an especially grateful heart for God's answers to prayer. Her name is Hannah, and we find her story in the Old Testament book of 1 Samuel.

Prayer in the Life of Hannah

In life, it's a good practice to stop and mark the special "firsts." Your first job. Your first house. Your first wedding anniversary. Your child's first steps. When you make an effort to pause and celebrate, to capture on film or to record the "firsts," they take on more meaning and can be recalled more easily again and again.

With the life and prayers of Hannah, we are presented with several important "firsts." In Hannah we have the first biblical record of extended prayer by a woman. It's true that Rebekah, the wife of Isaac, "went to inquire of the LORD." When her two unborn sons struggled in her womb, she asked God, "Why am I like this?" (Genesis 25:22). But with the introduction of Hannah and her prayers, we witness in great detail a devout woman's actions when faced with multiple and extreme difficulties.

As a bonus, we get a glimpse into Hannah's heart. We see her heart as she poured forth her concerns to God in prayer and also as she lifted praise to Him after her prayers were answered.

Hannah prayed with the right attitude—As the story of Hannah opens, we are immediately thrust into a domestic disaster—one man with two wives. And Hannah was one of those wives. She is described as barren, as a woman who "had no children," which was the worst possible failure for a married woman in the society of her day. To make matters worse, Hannah was regularly reminded of her failure by the taunts of her husband's other wife (1 Samuel 1:6).

Year after year, the ridicule directed at Hannah continued as the second wife gave birth to more and more children. But during the year described in 1 Samuel 1:3-19, when Hannah's husband, Elkanah, made the annual trip with his family to the tabernacle to make his peace offering, Hannah decided to do something about her problem. In heaviness of soul and with fasting (1:7), and after receiving only little comfort from her husband, Hannah went to the tabernacle to unburden her heart to God in prayer.

Have you ever heard the slogan "Attitude is everything"? And haven't you discovered this to be true in your own life? I know I have. My heart attitude definitely affects the way I approach any and every thing.

In Hannah's prayer, attitude was everything. She approached God in a spirit of humility. She didn't demand anything. She didn't even speak audibly. She just demonstrated a right attitude in her prayer as she spoke to God, referring to herself three times as "Your maidservant" (1:11). This title gives us a glimpse into Hannah's heart. She was a humble, submissive woman who came into the presence of her superior and sovereign God with a broken and contrite heart.

A Lesson to Learn about Prayer

We'll examine the life and prayers of Job in a few chapters. God allowed Job to endure—like Hannah—a number of physical, mental, and emotional trials in order to instill in him an important trait—in one word, *humility.* However, unlike Hannah, Job's initial attitude bordered on self-righteousness and pride. But with a little help from God, Job finally got the message. At last he said in brokenness, "I abhor myself, and repent in dust and ashes" (Job 42:6).

The lesson God taught Job was one of humility. And God used Hannah to model this same attitude—which you and I should also have when we approach our holy and sovereign God. Arguing in a spirit of arrogant pride is not the way to come to our Almighty God. His all-powerful position as our Creator and Father demands that our attitude be one of humility. Have you checked your heart attitude lately?

Hannah prayed in the right place—Since the beginning of the church age in the book of Acts, the Holy Spirit has indwelt believers. This means you and I can worship and pray to God in the Spirit, anywhere and at any time (John 4:24). But in Hannah's day, the Israelite men journeyed three times a year to the tabernacle in Shiloh to worship, offer sacrifices, and pray (Deuteronomy 16:1-17). In 1 Samuel 1, we read that Elkanah had brought his family to Shiloh for this observance. Therefore, Hannah was in the right place to meet with God.

Maybe the seriousness of Hannah's attitude was because of where she was—in the tabernacle, the earthly residence of God at that time. Yes, Hannah was serious. Rather than dwell on her problems and wallow in misery and self-pity, she determined to take her problem to God. Rather than retaliate against her husband or his spiteful other wife or give up hope, Hannah came to the only One who could heal her broken heart and take away the bitterness of her soul—to God Himself.

A Lesson to Learn about Prayer

Aren't you glad you don't have to take a 15-mile trip on foot to meet with God? That's what was required for Hannah to go to the tabernacle. Because of Jesus' perfect sacrifice on the cross, you don't have to make a trip to any special place to meet with God. Instead, you can worship the Father in the Spirit in any place and at any time. That's the good news!

The bad news is that you can sometimes take your unlimited and immediate access into the throne room of the Father for granted. It's too easy! The honor, respect, and passion for importuning God can be lost in the casualness of your everyday surroundings. Wherever you are, offer up your petitions with reverent confidence and anticipation...because wherever you pray, you *are* in the presence of a fully holy God. When you go to God in prayer, are you careful to remember that, no matter where you are, you are in the most holy tabernacle of God?

Hannah prayed in the right way—In a minute we'll discover what "the right way" is. But for now, let me say that there is no specific formula one must follow or position one must use in order to pray the right way. The Bible gives multiple examples of people bowing in prayer, kneeling in prayer, standing in prayer, even lying prostrate in prayer. Here are some of the different ways God's people prayed:

- Moses and Aaron—"fell on their faces" on many occasions as they offered up prayers and entreaties to God for the sins of the people (see Numbers 16:22 for one example).

- King David—meditated on his bed and wrote, "When I remember You on my bed, I meditate on You in the night watches" (Psalm 63:6).

- Solomon—knelt with his hands spread upward toward heaven as he offered a prayer of dedication for the newly completed temple (1 Kings 8:54).

- Jonah—prayed while in the stomach of a great fish (Jonah 2:1-9).

- Ezra—uttered his prayers for the people by "confessing,

weeping, and bowing down before the house of God" when
the people were unfaithful (Ezra 10:1).

- Nehemiah—prayed while standing on the wall and super-
  vising the workers: "We made our prayer to our God, and
  because of [the enemy] we set a watch against them day
  and night" (Nehemiah 4:9).

- Peter—prayed while walking on the water. Actually, he
  prayed, "Lord, save me!" while *sinking* in the water
  (Matthew 14:30).

- Paul—prayed on bended knee in prison while chained to
  guards: "For this reason, I bow my knees to the Father"
  (Ephesians 3:14).

- The Ephesian elders—knelt down on the beach and prayed
  with Paul before his last trip to Rome (Acts 20:36).

And Hannah? It appears she prayed to God for a son while
standing (1 Samuel 1:26). Nothing new here. This is a normal
and acceptable posture for prayer. But Hannah's prayer *was* different in one way. She "spoke in her heart; only her lips moved,
but her voice was not heard" (verse 13). This was highly unusual!
So unusual, in fact, that Eli, the priest, thought Hannah was drunk.
(And speaking of "firsts," Hannah's prayer in this manner is also
the first biblical record of silent or mental prayer.) Again, there
doesn't seem to be a specific way in which we *must* pray.

Now, getting back to my original statement that Hannah
prayed in "the right way," think about this: Regardless of her
posture, or whether she prayed out loud or silently, the fact that
Hannah prayed, and prayed with humility, was *the right way*.

A Lesson to Learn about Prayer

Realize there is no specific way we are expected to pray. So, if there are times when verbal prayer would help you express your thoughts and desires better, pray out loud to your heart's content. But also remember that words are not essential to the offering of true prayer. God listens to your heart as much as—or more than—to the words from your lips. Words are not always an accurate indicator of your true feelings, but your heart is. Your heart reveals your true self, and that is where God looks (1 Samuel 16:7). This is why you must "keep your heart with all diligence, for out of it spring the issues of life" (Proverbs 4:23).

You may experience times when even your heart doesn't know what to pray for or how. That's when the Spirit takes over and "makes intercession for us" (Romans 8:26).

And there will be times when, as with Hannah, your heart will be overflowing with thoughts and desires or hurts and confusion, to the point that verbal prayer is difficult. In these times, too, you can pray and let the Spirit help you in your weakness (Romans 8:26). After all, what is prayer? Isn't prayer the expression of your heart's sincere desires poured out to God, whether spoken or unspoken? What would you like to express to God right now?

Hannah prayed for the right result—At first glimpse, Hannah's prayer might be viewed as a very *selfish* prayer. She basically asked, "God, give me a child!" But was her plea really the selfish prayer of a barren mother facing a social stigma in her day? Could her prayer instead have been a prayer of selfless sacrifice? Read on for the answer.

Hannah's heartfelt request was followed by a sacrificial vow that showed her true character. In earnest, she petitioned, "O LORD of hosts, if You will indeed look on the affliction of Your maidservant and remember me, and not forget Your maidservant, but will give Your maidservant a male child, then I will give him to the LORD all the days of his life" (1 Samuel 1:11).

Hannah prayed for the right result...not for a child for herself, but a child for God! With resolute heart, she offered up her prayer as a vow to God that, in essence, said, "If You, God, will do this (give me a son), then I will do this (give him back to You)." In a sense, Hannah asked God for a loan—the loan of a son for about three years (1:24-28; 2:11).

A Lesson to Learn about Prayer

Hannah desired a result that would bless God's people and promote God's purposes. And her vow provides a sober warning: Be careful what you promise God in prayer. Why? Because God just might take you up on your vow.

Hannah was a desperate, barren woman for many years. But now the cloud of desperation that had focused her attention on what she wanted—a child—had been lifted. She now could set her own personal desires aside and focus her heart and mind on a more noble cause— that of glorifying God.

Many people pray with the wrong end in view. They

pray for health, wealth, and happiness, with themselves as the focus and beneficiary of the answers they seek. Make sure you pray for the right results—God's glory and His will. The right results come as you pray, "Not as I will, but as You will" (Matthew 26:39). What—and who—is the focus of your prayers?

Hannah prayed with the right response—How did God answer Hannah's first prayer? "It came to pass in the process of time that Hannah conceived and bore a son, and called his name Samuel" (1 Samuel 1:20).

In time, about three years later, after little Samuel had been weaned,[4] Hannah was ready to fulfill her vow. And she did so with a prayer. This prayer, recorded for us in 1 Samuel 2:1-10, is one of pure praise and thanksgiving. It reveals a heart of enormous gratitude.

Hannah's prayer of worship and thanksgiving expressed profound faith in God's power to keep His promises and joy at answered prayer. Her previous prayer was uttered in silence, but this prayer spoke forth a psalm of praise. And this time it was verbalized in the presence of Eli, who had earlier given his blessings on her silent prayer.

Hannah's humble prayer of gratitude is a significant mark of character in her life (2:1-10). Her utterance reveals an uncommon understanding of divine things. And this is even more remarkable when we consider that it was prayed at a time when Israel was led by the judges, a time when sin was rampant, for "there was no king in Israel; everyone did what was right in his own eyes" (Judges 21:25).

Hannah's prayer can be divided into several major themes about the Person of God:

- *God's salvation*—"I rejoice in Your salvation" (1 Samuel 2:1).

- *God's holiness*—"No one is holy like the LORD" (verse 2).

- *God's might*—"Nor is there any rock like our God" (verse 2).

- *God's understanding*—"The LORD is the God of knowledge" (verse 3).

- *God's power*—"The pillars of the earth are the LORD's, and He has set the world upon them" (verse 8).

- *God's care*—"He will guard the feet of His saints" (verse 9).

- *God's judgment*—"The adversaries of the LORD shall be broken in pieces" (verse 10).

With inspired understanding and ability, Hannah's heart expressed utmost faith in God's power and great joy over His answers to prayer. And emanating from within her mature knowledge of God's character is the element of total thankfulness! Prayerful gratitude forms a prominent characteristic of Hannah's heart, modeling a quality that is indispensable for experiencing an effective and fruitful prayer life. In the words of Charles Spurgeon, one of England's greatest preachers, "Thankfulness is not only an element of prayer; it will also be the end result of prayer: From prayer to praise is never a long or difficult journey."[5]

A Lesson to Learn about Prayer

Hannah praised God for His answer to her request for a son. She was thankful for who God is and what He had done and will always continue to do. She was confident of God's ultimate control over all events.

Like Hannah, you too can be confident of God's sovereign control of all things, including every aspect of your life. Therefore, you should be always and forever grateful for the many ways God blesses you and those you love and pray for. As you think on how God's power has sustained you in the past, you'll be strengthened and energized in your present difficulty. And in confidence and hope, you can look forward to His continued providence in your life in the future. How can you be more faithful to give thanks to God when He answers your prayers?

Hannah, a humble maidservant of the Lord, teaches us many lessons. But perhaps what stands out most vividly is her heart of gratitude. With unusually clear understanding Hannah saw God at work not only in her life, but also in all creation. Like Hannah, we should be thankful for the many ways God works in our lives. And by praising Him for His power and wisdom, we acknowledge His ultimate control over all the affairs of life—the good as well as the unpleasant. Therefore, in confidence, you may "in everything give thanks; for this is the will of God in Christ Jesus for you" (1 Thessalonians 5:18).

Prayer Principles for You—Gratitude

Prayer requires no manner or method.

Prayer is the heart's earnest desire, whether spoken or unspoken, and Hannah prayed both ways. You can think a prayer, speak a prayer, or sing a prayer. With prayer, it doesn't matter if you are in the grandest cathedral on earth or in the middle of nowhere. It doesn't matter if you are standing, kneeling, or prostrate on the ground. It doesn't matter what your manner or method is. What does matter is that you pray! Prayer is as essential to your spiritual life as exercise is to your physical life. "Prayer is the very life-breath of true Christianity."[6]

Prayer revives your joy.

Prayer has an amazing effect on your heart and soul. It transforms you from the inside out. If you pray about your sorrows, you are no longer sad. If you pray about your problems, they are supernaturally turned over to God. If you pray about your difficult life, you can face it and go on, even though nothing in your situation changes. Hannah poured out her heart to the Lord and received encouragement. She was revitalized with fresh joy and "went her way and ate, and her face was no longer sad" (1 Samuel 1:18). When you pray, you too will experience these same positive results, for the joy of the Lord is your strength (Nehemiah 8:10).

Prayer restores your trust.

You probably realize that every situation in your life is in God's hands. But do you ever wonder why sometimes you don't act like it, why you have doubts, why your faith gets rattled? Prayer is the secret weapon that restores your trust in God and reminds you that He will work out everything in your life for your good and His glory (Romans 8:28). Is there a crack in your trust in the Lord? Have any doubts slipped into your heart? Are you failing to trust Almighty God for the details of your life, your finances, your health, your family? Prayer will remove any fears and restore your trust. That's what happened to Hannah during her prayer time...and she walked away with complete faith that God had heard her and would act on her behalf.

Prayer releases your problems to God.

Through prayer you can release your problems to God, the "great problem solver." When you feel barren and fruitless, or when nothing seems to be going right in your life, your job, your family, or your ministry, pray. When you can't see your way out of a situation, pray. When you do, you will experience God's peace. Hannah prayed, releasing her problems to God, and returned home with peaceful contentment and waited patiently for God to work. Prayer helps end all your struggles because you've placed them in God's hands—which frees you to enjoy life.

Prayer results in peace of mind.

Are you enjoying the peace of mind prayer brings to the issues in your life? Life is hard, trying at the least. But God promises to satisfy the longing soul and to fill the hungry soul with His goodness (Psalm 107:9). When you suffer from bitterness of spirit and heart-wrenching misery, persevere in prayer. Only prayer can fill a hurting heart with joy, gratitude, and peace of mind. Hannah's prayers resulted in complete serenity, even as she gave up her beloved and only son. All was well with her soul.

A Prayer for Gratitude

Father, Your servant Hannah addressed You as "Lord of hosts"—as the One who commands the angelic armies of heaven. I come before You today, O Lord of hosts. You alone are the omnipotent deliverer of those who are suffering. Like Hannah, help me remember to turn to You with my problems when I or a loved one is in distress. And may I remember that my relationship with You also involves giving, not just receiving. After You graciously answered Hannah's prayer for a male child, she dedicated and delivered her son to You. I praise You now as I offer up to You the sacrifice of worship, gratitude, and thanksgiving. Amen.[7]

4

Prayers to Grow in Faithfulness

> *Moreover, as for me,*
> *far be it from me that I should sin*
> *against the LORD in ceasing to pray for you.*
>
> —1 SAMUEL 12:23

Before Charles Dickens drew the public's attention to the desperate plight of British orphans in his epic novel *Oliver Twist* (1837), George Muller became burdened to start a home for orphans in Bristol, England. Muller's vision began a most remarkable adventure of faith. He vowed to never ask for money, and he and his wife Mary lived by this principle for 40 years until her death. And George Muller continued praying and living totally by faith until his death 28 years later. Through the years, 18,000 children have been cared for and taught the truths of Scripture at this orphanage.

Described as one of the greatest prayer warriors of the past century, George Muller's life story is one of faithfulness in prayer. He dared to believe God could and would supply all of his personal needs *and* all the needs of the thousands of orphans he cared for during his lifetime. George Muller learned the secret of habitually praying for God's provision, and he practiced this spiritual exercise for much of his 93 years! He not only constantly asked God for physical provision, but he also asked for God's hand in spiritual provision.

In a specific instance of faithfulness in prayer, George Muller was deeply burdened for five of his friends who were not Christians. He began to steadfastly beseech God for their souls. Within five years, two of Muller's friends accepted Christ. Not giving up, he prayed for the next 20 years. One more became a Christian. Ever persistent, he kept asking God for the other men for nearly 40 years total until his death.[8] Both men became Christians within two years after his death. Needless to say, George Muller was a man of faithful prayer!

As we continue our look at knowing God through prayer, we come to another man who also showed great faithfulness in his prayer life. His name was Samuel, God's great prayer warrior, prophet, and priest.

What Does It Take to Be Great?

Do you ever wonder about the childhoods of the great and famous? What happened or didn't happen in their early years that formed the basis for their adult years of greatness? We can't know about all the greats, but the Bible contains a brief record of one great man—Samuel—and his beginnings. God has preserved the story of his ancestry, conception, and early years. Here's a thumbnail sketch—Samuel was:

—the son of Hannah, a woman of prayer.

—dedicated to God before he was conceived.

—"given" to God for service at about age three.

—a servant in the temple from his early childhood.

—responsive to God's call at an early age.

With a beginning like this we shouldn't be surprised to learn that little Samuel, the last judge in the time of the judges, was one of the greatest of the judges of Israel. His life of service to God provided a transition for God's people from being a nation lead by charismatic figures such as Moses, Joshua, and the judges to a nation ruled by kings. In fact, Samuel anointed the first two kings of Israel. So what made Samuel so special?

Clearly, Samuel was a man of prayer. His relationship with God was of such a nature that he inspired a whole nation to return to God and put away their idols. His spiritual strength became a nation's strength. The people drew confidence from Samuel because of his vital prayer life (1 Samuel 7:1-9).

But paired with Samuel's prayer life was the equally sterling quality of faithfulness in all things, especially in prayer. At one point in his relationship with the people, they feared that the godly Samuel would cease to pray for them because of their sin.

Samuel's often-quoted response shows us his heart and this quality of faithfulness: "Moreover, as for me, far be it from me that I should sin against the LORD in ceasing to pray for you" (12:23).

Samuel's commitment to prayer shows up again later after Saul was chosen to be Israel's first king. Saul repeatedly disobeyed God's commands, but Samuel wouldn't give up on him. After all, Samuel had anointed him king! He was faithful to pray and point Saul back toward God's instructions. Finally God asked Samuel, "How long will you mourn for Saul, seeing I have rejected him from reigning over Israel?" (16:1). God then sent Samuel to anoint David as the new king.

Prayer in the Life of Samuel

Was it prayer that motivated Samuel to faithfully follow God... or was it Samuel's faithful obedience that stimulated his prayer life? The answer is yes...and yes! Both traits—prayer and faithfulness—made up the inner fiber of this great man's life.

Let's begin here: How did a powerful prayer life and faithfulness make Samuel such a remarkable man of God? From the beginning of Samuel's life of service, God shows us through Samuel that faithfulness in the little things qualifies us to be trusted with greater things.

Samuel was faithful to respond to God's voice—Samuel was born at a time when Israel was constantly threatened by their archenemy, the Philistines. This was also an era of extreme moral darkness in Israel. It was a time when "the word of the LORD was rare" (3:1). God was silent. Therefore when God chose to speak to the young lad Samuel in the temple where he "ministered before the LORD, even as a child" (2:18), Samuel's confusion is understandable (3:1-9). It was Eli (the priest who was present when Samuel's mother, Hannah, prayed some 12 years before) who perceived that God was speaking to Samuel. And it was Eli who instructed Samuel to respond to God's voice, saying "Speak, LORD, for Your servant hears" (3:9).

A Lesson to Learn about Prayer

Samuel had a choice whether to believe or not believe Eli's perception that God was speaking to him, and that he should respond to this voice in the dark. Samuel chose to trust Eli's advice and to answer God's call. From that moment onward, God continued to speak and guide Samuel throughout his entire life.

In this day and age, God's voice comes to His people through His Holy Spirit as we read His Word in the Bible, and as we hear a sermon or the spoken wisdom of older, wiser believers. And, like Samuel, we have a choice of whether or not to respond as God speaks through various means. Learn well the lesson Samuel grasped at the beginning of his relationship with God. Learn to respond to God's voice and be willing to say, "Speak, for Your servant hears" (3:10).

Samuel was faithful to God's standards—Samuel the boy had several things going for him. First, he had a godly mother who poured God's truth into his soft little heart for his first three years of life. Following that, he had years of constant exposure to the things of God while ministering in the temple.

Then, in God's timing, God's man, Samuel, was ready for spiritual leadership. The people, too, were ready (7:2). So God thrust forth His servant Samuel to lead His people. When he stepped across that threshold, Samuel was in his thirties. Because of his own faithfulness, he could demand that the people repent and be faithful. Hear his challenge to God's people:

> If you return to the LORD with all your hearts,
> then put away the foreign gods...from among
> you, and prepare your hearts for the LORD, and
> serve Him only; and He will deliver you from
> the hand of the Philistines (7:3).

At this time, Samuel was about to have a significant impact on a whole nation—which makes this a good time to talk about the impact godly parents can have on a child during the first few formative years of life. Two men in the Bible had similar experiences as young children. Both Moses and now Samuel had been taught by faithful mothers. Both boys were separated from their parents by about age three. And both boys grew up to become spiritual leaders of God's people.

And note this too: Both men are linked together by God in Jeremiah 15:1 for their ability to intercede in prayer for others. We can never overestimate the influence of parents, and especially mothers, on their children when they are very young. The lives and impact of both Samuel and Moses should cause parents to think twice about "day care" over "mother's care."

A Lesson to Learn about Prayer

We are told very little about Samuel's early years with his mother and father. But reading Hannah's two famous prayers (1 Samuel 1:10-11; 2:1-10) should give us a clue as to his training. Don't you think that Hannah told her son the marvelous stories of God's love and care for His covenant people? And don't you think this godly mother prayed for her young son not only while she held him in her arms, but for all the years of her life when they were separated and he ministered far away in the temple?

The lesson for parents is evident: Praying for your children should be a lifelong vocation. Hannah dedicated her son to the Lord, and you can at least dedicate yourself to praying for your children—for their salvation, for their service to God, for wise choices of friends and godly mates, for the next generation of children to continue God's ministry. This may seem like a little thing, but it's a little thing that in time becomes a big thing as your children grow up and remain faithful to God's standards.

Samuel was faithful to pray for God's people—After the death of the priest, Eli, and his two sons, Samuel became the recognized spiritual leader and judge of the people. Accepting Samuel's challenge to repent (7:3), the people put away their idols (7:4). Next Samuel asked the people to gather at Mizpah, where he would pray for them (verse 5).

We don't know if Samuel had the ability to preach fiery sermons that moved and motivated the people of Israel. But we do know Samuel was recognized by the people as a man of prayer:

- The children of Israel said to Samuel, "Do not cease to cry out to the LORD our God for us." Then Samuel cried out to the Lord (verses 8-9).

- Samuel was displeased when the people said, "Give us a king to judge us." So Samuel prayed to the Lord (8:6).

- The people said to Samuel, "Pray for your servants to the LORD your God, that we may not die; for we have added to all our sins the evil of asking a king for ourselves" (12:19).

- "Moreover, as for me, far be it from me that I should sin against the LORD in ceasing to pray for you" (verse 23).

- "Now the word of the LORD came to Samuel...and he cried out to the LORD all night" (15:10-11).

Samuel regarded intercession as an integral part of his ministry. In Samuel's thinking, not to pray for his brethren was deemed a sin (12:23).

A Lesson to Learn about Prayer

The apostle James encourages us to "pray for one another" (James 5:16). Intercession through prayer is a powerful resource for a Christian. Don't do what many people do and use prayer only as a last resort after everything else has failed. Praying for others is a great privilege and also a great responsibility. God encourages us to intercede, and we can do so through prayer. Take a lesson from Samuel: Treat the lack of prayer for others as a sin against those who may very well need your prayers the most.

Samuel was faithful to seek God's help through prayer—Israel was in trouble. The Philistines had formed an army and started marching against Israel. The people were afraid and asked Samuel to pray for their deliverance (7:7-8).

Seeing their sensitive hearts as they worshiped and fasted (verse 6), Samuel faithfully took their concerns before the Lord. God responded to Samuel's prayer and the Philistines were routed, never to return to the territory of Israel during the life of Samuel (verses 9-13).

What an incredible turn of events! Chapter 7 of 1 Samuel begins in defeat...and ends with total deliverance. What a powerful tool Samuel possessed! A nation sought deliverance through the prayers of a man of God, and they were not disappointed... and God was glorified.

A Lesson to Learn about Prayer

Samuel is a good example of what we find mentioned in James 5:16: "The effective, fervent prayer of a righteous man avails much." Oh, man or woman of God, who better is there to handle the most difficult of problems than the God of all power (Ephesians 6:10)? The results of your prayers for others are often greater than you

think or imagine possible. God is able to do beyond all
you could ask or even think (Ephesians 3:20)! Don't let
the power of prayer for others go to waste. It's been said,
"A prayerless Christian is a powerless Christian." Don't be
a powerless Christian; be a praying Christian.

Samuel was faithful to continue to pray for God's people—
We've seen again and again that Samuel prayed for the people of
Israel. Intercession for others is a great privilege that we as
believers enjoy. Therefore, as children of the King, we shouldn't
hesitate to come boldly into the Father's throne room to seek His
grace and mercy for ourselves as well as our loved ones (Hebrews
4:16).

But where most of us have difficulty in interceding for others
is in praying for those who have hurt us or our family in some
way. We know we shouldn't act this way, so we struggle. Have you
ever been tempted to become cold or bitter toward someone
because of something they've done to you? Probably the last thing
you wanted to do was pray for them!

This happened to Samuel. Toward the end of his life, Samuel
faced the same dilemma. Briefly, here's the story: Samuel had faithfully served God's people for his entire life. Now he was an old man
(1 Samuel 8:1). Naturally, he wanted his sons to continue where he
left off in leading the people. But the elders came to him and pointed
out, "Your sons do not walk in your ways" (verse 5). Therefore, they
rejected Samuel's sons. Then, to make matters worse, the elders
wanted a king to lead them. They no longer wished to be led by
God in the traditional way God had established—through His

servants Moses, Joshua, the judges, and now Samuel. They wanted to be like the surrounding nations and have a king (verse 20).

How could the people do this to me? Samuel may have thought. *Sure, my sons have some problems. But isn't my faithful service enough to make up for their shortcomings?* We don't know what Samuel was thinking about his personal rejection, but we do know he was disappointed for God (8:6). He was jealous for God's honor.

During the era from Moses to Samuel, the Lord had been viewed as Israel's king. He was seen as the one the people could turn to when it was necessary to fight an enemy. So the call for a human king was an all-out rejection of God's rule. Samuel tried to convince the people that this was a bad idea. But in the end, and after prayer, God told Samuel to do as the people asked (verses 10-22).

Samuel could easily have slipped into a mode of indifference. He could have said, "They deserve whatever comes their way. If they won't listen, then I wash my hands of these people." But Samuel, our great man of faithfulness to God, to God's people, and to prayer, wasn't about to let the people and their foolish desires keep him from fulfilling his responsibilities.

As a last faithful act, Samuel addressed all the people at the coronation of their new king, Saul (12:1-15). By the time he finished speaking and God authenticated Samuel's message with thunder and rain, the people realized their sinful motives in wanting a king (verses 16-19). They needed Samuel to intercede for them. True to his commitment to the Lord and to the people, Samuel gave this great statement: "Moreover, as for me, far be it from me that I should sin against the Lord in ceasing to pray for you" (verse 23).

A Lesson to Learn about Prayer

Praying for your enemies or those who use and abuse you, or even those who foolishly disregard your advice, isn't usually the normal response, is it? But Jesus said that as a son or daughter of our Father in heaven, you are to "pray for those who spitefully use you and persecute you" (Matthew 5:44).

Samuel shows us that, in spite of how we are treated, you and I still need to pray faithfully for those around us. Let's not compound the sin of others by sinning ourselves in failing to pray for others—including our enemies.

Samuel was faithful to follow God to the end—From the very beginning of Samuel's many years of service in the temple, when God told him as an adolescent to deliver a harsh word of rebuke to Eli (1 Samuel 3:11-14), until the end of his life, Samuel showed a spiritual fitness that qualified him to discern God's will and Word. This is especially evident when Samuel was asked by God to perform one last official act—to go to the house of Jesse in Bethlehem and anoint a new king.

In Samuel's mind there was just one problem: Israel still had a king by the name of Saul. In his human spirit, Samuel initially hesitated. "How can I go? If Saul hears it, he will kill me" (16:2). But true to the spiritual fitness that he gained through prayer and faithfulness, the Bible reports, "So Samuel did what the LORD said, and went to Bethlehem" (verse 4).

A Lesson to Learn about Prayer

A particular feature of God's replies to the prayers of Old Testament saints is that His voice seemed to fall on the inner ear or mind like the voice of a man. This phenomenon is evidenced in the last scene from the life of Samuel as he "dialogued" with God in the choice of David as the new king (16:1-12).

Recall again that God has provided numerous ways for His people to "hear" His leading and respond in obedience. The lesson you and I need to learn from this dialogue between God and Samuel is this: Even though Samuel initially hesitated, he "listened" to God through prayer and ultimately followed God's command. So the question is, are you presently hesitating to follow God's direction because it seems too difficult or impossible? Follow in Samuel's footsteps. Pray...and then do what the Lord guides you to do. God will be honored, His will will be accomplished, and you will be blessed as you faithfully obey.

Samuel marked the end of an era, the last of his kind. In a sense he was the spiritual glue that held the young nation of Israel together as it moved forward in development. Samuel's life was also a testament to faithfulness:

- Samuel was faithful to Eli as a student

- Samuel was faithful to God as a servant

- Samuel was faithful to the people as a steward of God's truths

- Samuel was faithful to pray as a steward of God's people

May you and I follow in the faithful praying footsteps of Samuel and be counted along with him as faithful "stewards of the mysteries of God" (1 Corinthians 4:1-2).

Prayer Principles for You—Faithfulness

Prayer is a spiritual exercise for all ages.

At what age can a person begin talking to God? At the same age they begin to talk to their parents. Prayer is simply talking to God. Little Samuel responded to God by simply speaking to Him. No matter what your age or what you do or don't know about prayer, or whether you did or didn't have parents who taught you to pray, you can participate in the spiritual exercise of prayer. How? By beginning now, today, this minute, to simply talk to God. It's also never too early to teach your children to talk to God in prayer. Help them develop their sensitivity to spiritual things and pray that one day, in childlike obedience, they will respond to God's call on their life with "Speak, for Your servant hears" (1 Samuel 3:10).

Prayer changes things.

Prayer changes things. And prayer changes people, too. Thanks to God and to the prayerful influence of Samuel, the revival that started in the hearts of God's people in Samuel's day lasted for more than 100 years. Do you need any changes in your life? A revival? Prayer is an acknowledgment of your dependence on God and His direction for your life. Therefore the more you pray, the more you are stating your desire to live your life by God's standards. You can't help but be transformed as you pray, "Not my will, but Your will be done."

Prayer requires a pure heart.

Think about this true story: At the end of his life, Samuel asked the people to evaluate his life and ministry. Their response was an overwhelming acknowledgment that Samuel had not cheated anyone, bribed anyone, stolen from anyone, or oppressed anyone (1 Samuel 12:3-4). In other words, Samuel was blameless in his dealings with the people. His heart was pure. This condition contributed to his being an effective prayer warrior and a vessel through whom God could work powerfully.

How's your heart? Have you had a checkup lately? Because effective prayer requires a pure heart, take seriously the admonition of the psalmist: "If I regard iniquity in my heart, the Lord will not hear" (Psalm 66:18). Confession of sin and a love for God results in a pure life. Then what happens? "The effective, fervent prayer of a righteous man [or woman] avails much" (James 5:16).

Prayer is the privilege of all believers.

No one will ever understand how prayer works into the plans of a sovereign God. But we can know and believe that somehow it does. God, in His wisdom, has determined that your prayers are a part of His grand scheme of things. What a privilege! So determine to pray faithfully for other believers. The apostle Paul told believers that he never ceased to pray for them. He also asked other believers to pray for him and his missionary team and for the Word of the Lord to be glorified.[9]

You have the privilege of being able to enter into the sovereign plan of God. Why not exercise your privilege and be part of God's work in His world?

Prayer is the responsibility of all believers.

With every privilege comes responsibility. Samuel assumed the full weight of his responsibility to pray, and so should we. The Bible tells us to pray for those who hurt us, for God to send forth laborers into His harvest, for the sick, for one another, to watch and pray without ceasing. God asks—and expects—us to accept our responsibility and pray. Pray regularly...and may God give you an even greater desire!

A Prayer for Faithfulness

Lord, Samuel addressed You as "LORD" when he responded to Your call to serve Him. He was a young boy, and yet he answered Your call, saying, "Speak...for Your servant hears." As a faithful servant to You, Lord, Samuel listened with an obedient heart when You called. May I also be one who listens with a desire to obey, and not be a person who merely hears Your Word and does nothing. May I recall and heed Samuel's words to King Saul: "To obey is better than sacrifice." My prayer is that I will "delight to do Your will, O my God." Amen.[10]

5

Prayers to Grow in Trust

O LORD my God, in You I put my trust;
save me from all those who persecute me;
and deliver me.

—PSALM 7:1

Hundreds of years ago, the leaders of Florence, Italy, commissioned a sculptor to create a magnificent work of art for their city square. To ensure the beauty of the statue, they purchased the most expensive marble available. Demanding privacy, the sculptor hammered and chiseled away. Finally the day arrived for the unveiling. The citizens were shocked and disgusted with the hideous creation. The disappointing piece of marble was hauled off to the city dump, and the sculptor slipped out of town and was quickly forgotten.

Years later, another artist, young and unknown, came to Florence. He was hired to work on the discarded stone. After months of painstaking work, the resurrected piece of stone was again placed in the city square. The unknown artist was Michelangelo, and the work of art that was re-created is his statue of the Old Testament hero, David, considered to be one of the most exquisite and priceless figures in all the fields of sculpture and art.

Michelangelo's statue of David is an example of what a master craftsman can do even with a piece of rock discarded by others. And centuries before the statue of David was sculpted, we witness what God, the Master Sculptor, did with the man who inspired the great masterpiece—David himself. He was a man whose heart was truly committed to trusting his God. He was a man after God's own heart (1 Samuel 13:14). As a result of David's trust in God, God was able to use him mightily.

Trusting the Lord

From the beginning of what the biblical record tells us about David, we are aware of his heart for God and his understanding of the nature of God. All through his life, David had complete trust in God. Whether as a shepherd boy protecting his father's flock from lions and bears, as a lad with five stones defending God's honor against the giant Goliath, or as a warrior advancing Israel's borders through victory, David trusted in God. His heart for God is also seen throughout the many psalms he wrote. He was as much a poet as he was a warrior and was referred to as the "sweet psalmist of Israel" (2 Samuel 23:1).

Unfortunately, even though David had a heart for God, he allowed sin to creep into his life, and it produced disastrous consequences. His life and family were never the same after his sin with Bathsheba. It looked like David was done!

But, like the great sculptor Michelangelo, who refashioned a discarded piece of marble, God, the Greatest Sculptor, took David's destroyed life and refashioned him and again made him His magnificent and useful servant.

Prayer in the Life of David

Several books and many chapters of the Bible must be read if you want to know the details of David's life.[11] But if you want to know what was happening in David's heart as a result of what was happening in his life, then you must read his prayers and his psalms. In these prayers of the heart, David pours forth his soul to God. He chronicles his hopes, fears, triumphs, disappointments, and labors. And many of David's prayers end on a note of singular trust in the powerful and sustaining hand of God.

The sampling of prayers we'll consider here are representative of the life and psalms of David. They give us an understanding of what a remarkable man of prayer he was.

David trusted God—Soon after David was anointed to be king, he was summoned before the current king, Saul, to calm Saul's troubled spirit with music. David was selected because he was "skillful in playing." But he was also handpicked because those at Saul's court had reported, "The LORD is with him" (1 Samuel 16:18). David's growing relationship with God was already being noticed by others.

In the very next chapter we see David in the middle of a

national crisis, fighting the giant Goliath (1 Samuel 17)! David was probably just a teenager, but by default, he confidently volunteered to fight a seasoned warrior who had put fear into the hearts of all the men and warriors of Israel. No prayers were uttered in this scene. But we have to believe that much previous prayer and worship had contributed to young David's bold and fearless decision to take on a giant who was nine feet and nine inches tall, and wore armor weighing 125 pounds![12]

What motivated David to go up against impossible odds? It was his concern for God's honor and reputation. David asked incredulously, "Who is this uncircumcised Philistine, that he should defy the armies of the living God?" (verse 26).

David had trusted God in the past against lions and bears. Now David was confident he could trust God to give him victory in the present, especially since Goliath was an enemy of Israel and of God (verse 36). Holding only a slingshot and a few rocks, David defiantly shouted forth his trust in God to the giant, "The battle is the LORD's, and He will give you into our hands" (verse 47).

A Lesson to Learn about Prayer

Crisis comes to us in a myriad of ways—a call from the doctor, a runaway child, a dissolved marriage, a death. When the crisis comes, and come it will, how will you face it? David chose to face his nation's crisis head on.

How could this lad, perhaps only 18 years old, step forward when thousands of grown men and soldiers had stepped backward? David's decision points to a personal history of prayer, worship, and faith. He needed prayer for the courage to challenge the giant. He needed a heart of worship to recognize this was a spiritual battle, not a physical one. And he needed a well-exercised faith to trust God for yet another victory—an impossible-without-God victory!

Don't wait for a crisis to come before you develop your prayer life. Don't wait for a tragedy to strike before you begin to exercise your faith. And don't wait to be told that you are in a spiritual battle before you worship. Follow David's example and his prayerful advice: "To You, O LORD, I lift up my soul. O my God, I trust in You" (Psalm 25:1).

David sought God's direction—David was a powerful warrior and a great military leader. But a good part of his success, especially in the early years, came because he sought the Lord's direction. Note these instances:

- Before attacking the Philistines at Keilah, "David inquired of the LORD" (1 Samuel 23:2).

- Before pursuing a band of Amalekites who had attacked his camp, "David inquired of the LORD" (30:8).

- Before moving into the cities of Israel and proclaiming himself as king, David "inquired of the LORD," and the Lord said "Go up." Then David asked, "Where shall I go up?" and God told him to go up "to Hebron" (2 Samuel 2:1).

David often experienced reciprocal communication with God: He would ask...and God would answer. Seven times we read that "David inquired of the LORD." And every time David did, he experienced success. Imagine, a 100-percent success rate! But sadly, every time David failed to consult with God about a matter, he experienced failure and ended up doing rash and often sinful things—giving him a 100-percent rating in the opposite direction.

A Lesson to Learn about Prayer

This is a recurring lesson, isn't it? It goes something like this: If you are to remain in God's will, you must continually seek God's will. You must consult with God before you act, react, or respond. You must not try to scheme or manipulate your way through life. Instead, you should consult God through prayer and the study of His Word.

Before you make another decision, "inquire of the LORD." You and everyone else will be glad you did!

David thirsted for God—When God first chose David to replace King Saul, He declared, "I have found David...a man after My own heart, who will do all My will" (Acts 13:22). David was far from perfect. He had his ups and downs. But throughout most of his life, David followed after God, praying prayers such as, "O God, You are my God; early will I seek You; my soul thirsts for You; my flesh longs for You" (Psalm 63:1-2).

A Lesson to Learn about Prayer

What's the temperature of your heart? Have you checked it lately? Hopefully your heart is warm and sensitive toward God. But a word of caution comes to us from David's life: Today's godly attitudes come with no guarantee that you will be this kind of person with this kind of heart five, ten, or twenty years from now. Pray daily that God will help you keep your heart hot—keep it hungering and thirsting after Him.

David understood the value of time—I once read about a man who had a calendar made for himself that counted backward from a projected date in the future based on a calculation of his life expectancy. He was taking Moses' admonition very seriously, "Teach us to number our days, that we may gain a heart of wisdom" (Psalm 90:12). He was literally "numbering his days."

Like Moses in Psalm 90 and like this man, David also showed his concern for the value of his time on this earth when he prayed, "LORD, make me to know my end, and what is the measure of my days, that I may know how frail I am. Indeed, You have made my days as handbreaths" (Psalm 39:4-5).

David's abiding relationship with God gave him an accurate picture of his life. A *handbreath* is the width of the hand at the base of the four fingers.[13] That's only a little over three inches. The Bible, and David, are saying life is short—just a few inches long in relation to eternity.

A Lesson to Learn about Prayer

Prayer allows you to build an abiding relationship between you and your heavenly Father. As you pray, you slip into the eternal realm of the Father, where the cares and desires of this world take on a heavenly perspective. Through prayer your life is seen not only for its value in time, but also for its value throughout all eternity.

Life is short! So follow David's example and ask God to help you better grasp the value of your time and its importance for eternity. Ask God to give you a heart of wisdom to live your life in the best way. Ask Him to help you use your time wisely, to prioritize your tasks and goals in life, to understand that time lost will never be regained.

David asked for forgiveness—When God called David "a man after My own heart," He wasn't suggesting David was perfect. Most of the time David was successful, but like us, there were times when he stumbled and fell. It's in these instances we realize that a passion for the Lord will help in the battle against sin, but by itself it will not keep us from sinning. We are men and women of a fleshly nature (Romans 7:18), and therefore we are at all times susceptible to falling into sin. And a passion for God will help bring us back to God when we fail.

This was true in David's terrible sin with Bathsheba. It took a while (about a year—2 Samuel 12:14), but, as David's prayer for forgiveness reveals, he did ultimately express a deep sense of guilt: "I acknowledged my sin to You, and my iniquity I have not hidden. I said, 'I will confess my transgression to the LORD'" (Psalm 32:5).

In time David also wrote a confession—Psalm 51—and handed it over to "the Chief Musician" to be used in public worship. The superscription at the beginning of the psalm bluntly describes the occasion of its writing: "A Psalm of David when Nathan the prophet went to him, after he had gone in to Bathsheba." In this prayer, David took full responsibility for his actions: "I acknowledge my transgressions, and my sin is always before me. Against You, You only, have I sinned, and done this evil in Your sight" (verses 3-4).

In deep repentance, David trusted in God's grace as he cried out, "Create in me a clean heart, O God, and renew a steadfast spirit within me" (verse 10). David had always enjoyed a close and vital relationship with God. However, when he sinned, that joy was lost. Therefore he prayed to God to "restore to me the joy of Your salvation" (verse 12).

A Lesson to Learn about Prayer

Confession of sin is an admission of fault. In our prayers of confession we agree with God that we have violated His standards, and ask to be restored to a right relationship with Him...which restores our joy.

We learn at least two lessons from David's prayers of confessions: First, we need to make sure we are quick to take responsibility for our actions and confess them. And second, we must be quick to ask for forgiveness so our walk with God is restored and the burden of unconfessed sin doesn't consume us. God is always there, and He is always faithful to forgive (1 John 1:9).

David had an understanding of God—From an early age, David was responsive to God's self-revelation. God declared him to be "a man after My own heart" while David was a mere teenager. His responsiveness to know God and eagerness to glorify Him is demonstrated throughout David's prayers and psalms, especially in Psalm 139. Here, David gives us the heights and the depths of his understanding of God's character.

- God is omniscient—He knows our every thought (verses 1-6).

- God is omnipresent—He is everywhere and we cannot hide from Him (verses 7-12).

- God is omnipotent—He is all-powerful and the creator of all things, including you and me (verses 13-16).

- God is loving—He is concerned with the details of our lives and the condition of our hearts (verses 17-24).

David's dynamic and intimate relationship with God shaped his perspective on life. He knew that he wasn't alone, that God was always with him. Therefore David trusted God with his life and his soul. We see this trust evidenced in David's prayer in Psalm 139: "Search me, O God, and know my heart; try me, and know my anxieties; and see if there is any wicked way in me" (verses 23-24). Do you wonder what made David's vital relationship with God possible? Maybe it was his willingness to expose himself to God's purifying gaze. In this prayer, David essentially gave God the keys to his heart, leaving nothing hidden and no part of his life inaccessible to God.

A Lesson to Learn about Prayer

How we act in life is determined by how well we know and respond to God. When we have a right view of God, our understanding will lead to right conduct. David was continually responsive to God's revelation of Himself—whether while tending his father's sheep, or while being tested by King Saul's frequent attempts to kill him. All of life afforded David the opportunity to grow in his understanding of God. His willingness to allow his life to be an open book before God through prayer also enhanced his maturing process.

Are your prayers a reflection of a growing relationship with God? Is your life an open book? Can you pray along with David, "Search me, O God, and know my heart... and see if there is any wicked way in me"?

David prayed from a grateful heart—A common theme in the lives of the powerful men and women of the Bible is their gratitude. Their prayers were filled with thanks to God for His blessings.

- Hannah prayed, "My heart rejoices in the LORD; My horn is exalted in the LORD....I rejoice in Your salvation" (1 Samuel 2:1-2).

- Nehemiah and the elders of Israel expressed their thanks and gratitude to God by praying, "You are God, gracious and merciful" (Nehemiah 9:31).

- Daniel "knelt down on his knees three times [a] day and prayed and gave thanks before his God" (Daniel 6:10).

- Mary broke forth in praise and thanksgiving at God's choice of her as the vessel to bring the Messiah into the world: "My soul magnifies the Lord, and my spirit has rejoiced in God my Savior" (Luke 1:46-49).

David, Mary's distant relative, had much to be thankful for... and he was faithful to express gratefulness. Perhaps his most famous prayer of gratitude was offered up to God as he "sat before the Lord" after being told God was making an everlasting covenant with him and his house (2 Samuel 7:12-16). Overwhelmed by gratitude, he prayed, "Who am I, O Lord GOD? And what is my house, that You have brought me this far?" (verse 18).

A Lesson to Learn about Prayer

As a child of the King, you have much to be thankful for. God has given you "every spiritual blessing in the heavenly places in Christ" (Ephesians 1:3). Every waking moment should be spent in a prayerful attitude of gratitude. Even on those dark days when life seems to be crashing in on you, don't give in to despair. Do as David did—worship God and pray and pour out thanksgiving to Him. God is in control, and you can gratefully leave everything—even the bad things—in the powerful and capable hands of God.

David was one of the greatest men of the Old Testament—a shepherd, a poet, a giant-killer, a king, a man of prayer, and an ancestor of Jesus Christ. But he was also an adulterer and a murderer. The Bible paints both pictures of David's life with vivid color and bold strokes. Nothing is hidden.

So what is it that made David such a remarkable man of God, a man after God's own heart? David had an unwavering trust in God's ability to forgive his sin, to protect him from his enemies, and to provide for his family and the nation. This trust was particularly evident at the spiritual level—David trusted in the faithful and forgiving nature of God, and ultimately trusted God for his eternal destiny.

The sweet psalmist of Israel and man after God's own heart never took God's forgiveness nor his relationship with God lightly. David's faith and trust in God never diminished. It grew stronger until his last days. After all, he was the man who wrote,

> Yea, though I walk through the valley of the shadow of death, I will fear no evil; for You are with me....Surely goodness and mercy shall follow me all the days of my life; and I will dwell in the house of the LORD forever (Psalm 23:4,6).

Prayer Principles for You—Trust

Prayer gives you the right perspective.

It's easy to get caught up in and be distracted by the things of this world. As a result, you can become defeated by what appear to be limited solutions. You can lose sight of the bigger picture.

Prayer helps you keep a solid footing in the world as you do heavenly business. Without a vital prayer life you can become one-dimensional, seeing things only from a limited earthly perspective. But when you pray, you see life more from a limitless heavenly perspective. David sought to view life from heaven's vista. He wanted to do nothing but follow after God's heart. Therefore, he prayed.

Prayer sharpens your perspective on the value of your time and clarifies the direction God wants you to go. Prayer also brings God to the forefront of your problems and increases your trust in Him.

Prayer should permeate your day.

In Psalm 55:17, David wrote, "Evening and morning and at noon I will pray, and cry aloud." David was a man who prayed as often as needed. Follow David's example, and allow prayer to invade every hour and every action of your day. Is your soul less thirsty for the living God? Refresh and revive it through prayer. Is time speeding by and there's little to show for it? Ask God for a fresh vision for the days of your life. Do you need forgiveness? Pray on the spot. Do you lack wisdom about something? Ask for it. Do you need to speak to someone about an issue? Pray first. Is your trust in God wavering? Bolster it by praying. Let prayer permeate your every day and your every concern.

Prayer exhibits an attitude of trust.

When you pray, you are trusting God for the outcome. That's an attitude. David had an attitude of total trust in God's hand to superintend his life. In Psalm 31, he prayed, "In you, O LORD, I put my trust....Be my rock of refuge, a fortress of defense to save me....I trust in the LORD. I will be glad and rejoice in Your mercy....I trust in You, O LORD...You are my God....My times are in Your hand; deliver me from the hand of my enemies, and from those who persecute me" (verses 1-2,6-7,14-15).

How's your attitude? Are you expressing your trust in God for all the details of your life? He's your rock of refuge, too, and your fortress of defense!

Prayer should be simple.

Sincere prayer should be uncomplicated. God listens to and hears the prayers of a child and a theologian alike. Most of David's prayers were simple, heartfelt petitions: "O LORD....You understand my thought....Deliver me, O LORD, from evil men.... Make haste to me! Give ear to my voice when I cry out to You."[14]

When you pray from your heart as David did, then your prayers will be simple and passionate. The most impressive prayers are those that express one's needs with sincerity and simplicity. Pray like the tax collector who, "standing afar off, would not so much as raise his eyes to heaven, but beat his breast, saying, 'God, be merciful to me a sinner!'" (Luke 18:13). Seven simple words, but the seven most powerful words any man or woman can ever utter!

A Prayer for Trust

O Great Shepherd, I rejoice in knowing that, like David, I can trust in You as "my shepherd." David discovered that You, as a shepherd, are a guide, protector, and constant companion to Your flock. Help me to remember that at all times and in every circumstance—even during dark days or when the valley of the shadow of death approaches—I can trust You. I can trust that You are near. I can trust that You are my rock and my salvation. Blessed be Your holy name! Amen.[15]

6

Prayers to Grow in Purpose

*Please let Your ear be attentive and Your eyes open,
that You may hear the prayer of Your servant
which I pray before You now, day and night.*

—Nehemiah 1:6

W*hat is my purpose?*
The vast majority of the world's people are asking this question. They are wondering, *Why am I here? What is the meaning of life? What should I do with my life?* And these questions span across all age and intellectual boundaries. High-school seniors and senior citizens—and everyone in between —are asking about purpose. Philosophers with brilliant minds and Ph.D. degrees have been debating the question of purpose since the beginning of recorded history.

Sadly, Christians are asking these same questions. Yet if we would just read our Bibles, we (and that includes me, too) would begin to understand our purpose. And that understanding would transform our lives. Here's how Rick Warren states this idea of purpose in his extremely popular book, *The Purpose-Driven Life:*

> The purpose of your life is far greater than
> your own personal fulfillment, your peace of
> mind, or even your happiness. It's far greater
> than your family, your career, or even your
> wildest dreams and ambitions.[16]

Warren goes on to tell us where we must start: "If you want to know why you were placed on this planet, you must begin with God. You were born by his purpose and for his purpose."[17]

Purpose Begins with God

So, as Rick Warren has observed, if we want to recognize our purpose, we must "begin with God." We must begin by submitting our lives to be used by God for His purposes.

This is what happened to a man who lived some 400-plus years before Christ. His name was Nehemiah, and his story is told in the book of the Bible that bears his name. As we look at his life, you'll notice the role prayer played in his discovery of God's purpose for him.

Nehemiah was a very successful man. He was an important and trusted official in the Persian Empire. As a "cupbearer" to the king (Nehemiah 1:11), Nehemiah made sure that nothing harmful was ever given to the king to eat or drink. His position made him one of only a few men who had direct access to the king. For a foreigner—a Jew—Nehemiah had it made!

But one day something happened that would turn his life upside down, that would change his desires forever. A fellow Jew from Jerusalem, the ancient capital of the Jews which had been destroyed by the Babylonians, reported that the "survivors...are there in great distress and reproach. The wall of Jerusalem is also broken down, and its gates are burned with fire" (verse 3). This message was so dismaying that Nehemiah "sat down and wept, and mourned for many days" (verse 4). He immediately started "fasting and praying before the God of heaven" (verse 4).

Now I ask you, what is your reaction when you hear tragic news? It's only natural to react in the same way Nehemiah did. A loved one has died, your heart is broken, so you cry and mourn. Some needless tragedy occurs, so you are distraught and perplexed. But do you take the next needed step? Do you do like Nehemiah did and start praying before the God of heaven? Do you immediately go to God to seek His will and to gain an understanding of what He is allowing to happen in your life? Turning to God in prayer is the starting point for handling all of life if we want to figure out what is happening to us.

Now, let's see how beginning with God in prayer helped Nehemiah find his purpose.

Prayer in the Life of Nehemiah

Nehemiah was neither a prophet nor a priest, but he was a Jew who knew God and loved Him. Even though he was hundreds of miles away from his homeland, he knew the significance of

Jerusalem to God. He was also greatly distressed that more than 90 years after the return of many captives, Jerusalem still was not rebuilt, and more importantly, the cause of God had not progressed.

With this historical information as a background, you and I are now privileged to listen in on several of Nehemiah's prayers. As we will soon discover, God, and seeking God's direction, was the constant habit of this remarkable man.

Nehemiah prayed for direction—As we saw earlier, Nehemiah was greatly shaken by the news from Jerusalem. How could he help? Being hundreds of miles away, what could he do?

One thing Nehemiah could do was pray. He could come before God with a humble submissive heart. And that's what he did. He shows us how to approach God:

—Nehemiah began his prayer with fasting and reverential worship and adoration:
  O great and awesome God (Nehemiah 1:5).

—Nehemiah then reminded God of His covenant and promise. He prayed:
  You...keep Your covenant and mercy with those who love You and observe Your commandments (verse 5).

—Nehemiah next brought confession into his prayer. He included himself in his confession of sins—both his and the sins of his fellow Jews:
  We have sinned against You....We have acted very corruptly against You, and have not kept the commandments, the statutes, nor the ordinances which You commanded Your servant Moses (verses 6-7).

—Nehemiah further, in full confidence, asked God to remember His word to Moses—a word of retribution for the disobedient and redemption for the obedient (verses 8-9).

—Nehemiah at last began to sense God's direction and the part he must set about to play in fulfilling God's purpose. God's guidance and purpose grew out of his awareness of the need and his understanding of God's nature as he immersed himself in prayer before he approached King Artaxerxes with a request:
Let Your servant prosper this day, I pray, and grant him mercy in the sight of this man (verse 11).

A Lesson to Learn about Prayer

My praying friend, God is the God of the brokenhearted. Nehemiah was distraught and helpless. What could he do to assist his people? He could pray. So, like Nehemiah, who prayed out of distress and concern, what worry or pain or need can you take to God in prayer? Nehemiah appealed to the promises of God for His people. What promise from God can you claim during your hour of need? Why not take your promise to God in prayer and seek to determine the role He would have you play in His great plan and His purpose for you?

Nehemiah prayed on the spot—Nehemiah continued in prayer for four months.[18] And in the process of performing his duties—giving wine to the king—the king asked what was causing Nehemiah to be sad. Sadness was a dangerous emotion to express in the presence of this king, and Nehemiah feared for his life.

Nehemiah had no time to shut his eyes or bend his knee and spend a prolonged time in prayer. He had only a split second to offer up a quick prayer for assistance: "So I prayed to the God of heaven" (2:4). (This reminds me of another quick prayer, which was offered up by Jesus' disciple, Peter, when he was sinking while walking on water: "Lord save me" [Matthew 14:30]. There is obviously a time for spontaneous, urgent prayer.)

Because Nehemiah was in the habit of praying regularly, his natural response to this dangerous situation was to offer up a quick, silent "arrow prayer." Instinctively he asked God for wisdom and direction, and God rewarded through an abundant response from the king. Because Nehemiah had been praying extensively for months about the situation in Jerusalem, he was able to boldly ask for a leave of absence, supplies for the rebuilding of the wall, and protection for the journey (Nehemiah 2:4-8).

Nehemiah had found his purpose! But in the eyes of society, this new direction was a definite demotion. Nehemiah was leaving one of the most powerful positions in the empire for a governorship in Jerusalem, considered to be a backwater district in a forgotten part of the empire. But none of this mattered to Nehemiah. He had found his purpose through prayer. And he was compelled to follow God's plan for his life, regardless of the cost.

A Lesson to Learn about Prayer

Wherever we are, we have a way to heaven open to us. It's prayer. Whether at work or at home, while traveling, or whatever we are doing in our hectic lives, we can silently express our needs and desires to the God of heaven on the spot. We can follow Nehemiah's example and offer up silent, spontaneous prayers hundreds of times a day. Nehemiah provides us with a perfect illustration of the attitude of mind that believes that, in any and all circumstances, we can practice the presence of God by talking to Him through prayer, whether in an "arrow prayer" or in our prayer closet.

Nehemiah prayed for deliverance—Nehemiah now had a vision, a purpose. But he couldn't fulfill it alone. When he arrived in Jerusalem and surveyed the destruction, he realized he needed others to join him in this grand purpose—that of rebuilding the wall to counter the reproach on God's people and God's name. So, through an impassioned speech, he won the support of the people, and they began—together—to rebuild the city wall (verses 17-18).

But as Nehemiah and the people proceeded to act on God's purpose, opposition reared its ugly head and tried seven times to stop the progress.[19] What did Nehemiah do? You guessed it! Scripture records that in response to most of the enemies' attempts to disrupt the building, Nehemiah prayed. He prayed that God would thwart the evil schemes and judge the evil men who were attempting to stop the work of God: "Hear, O our God... turn their reproach on their own heads, and give them as plunder to a land of captivity" (4:4).[20]

A Lesson to Learn about Prayer

Nehemiah believed in what he was doing. He believed he was doing the work of God in rebuilding the wall. And he believed that the persecution was coming as a result of that work. So his prayers for deliverance were not for his own welfare but for the welfare of the workers, for the building of the wall, and for the glory of God. The next time you feel persecuted and are ready to pray for deliverance, ask yourself the reason for the persecution. Is it because of some character issue in your life that people are reacting to, or is it because of the work of God and His glory? If it's the latter, pray on!

Nehemiah prayed for restitution—The work on the wall was progressing in spite of hassles from the enemy outside the wall. But a new problem arose. It was the enemy within the walls! The enemy was greed. Many of the nobles and the wealthy did not support the reconstruction (3:5), probably because of their ties with men who were enemies of God and His purposes (2:19-20). The wealthy class exploited the poor of the city by charging excessive interest (5:7). This made it impossible for the people to repay their loans. The result was that many families were sold into slavery.

Responding to the cries of the people, Nehemiah demanded that the nobles restore what was taken from the poor. Then to show that he meant business, Nehemiah visually shook his garment, prayed for restoration to the impoverished, and called down God's wrath upon anyone who failed to follow through on their promise to release the debts, uttering, "So may God shake out each man...who does not perform this promise" (verse 13).

Nehemiah didn't take advantage of the people (verses 14-18), and he expected the nobles to do the same.

A Lesson to Learn about Prayer

God's concern for the poor is expressed in almost every book of the Bible. God never intended for people to profit from the misfortunes of others. Nehemiah held the nobles to God's standard of caring for the poor. Today, we too should be prayerfully on the lookout for fellow believers who need our helping hand or who are being taken advantage of. We may not be in a leadership position like Nehemiah was, where we can demand restitution or relief for others. But we can always pray for opportunities to help those who are less fortunate.

Four hundred years later, in this very same city, the Jerusalem church was praised for working together to reduce poverty (Acts 4:34-35). May we and our present-day churches follow this example and make it a practice to pray about ways to help those in need. Remember, "he who gives to the poor will not lack" (Proverbs 28:27). And don't worry about your own needs. "God shall supply all your need according to His riches in glory by Christ Jesus" (Philippians 4:19).

Nehemiah prayed in confession—Through prayer and diligence, the wall was at last completed—in only 52 days (Nehemiah

6:15)! So, in a spirit of celebration, the people spontaneously gathered in the open square and asked that the Book of the Law of Moses be brought out and read to them. As the Book of the Law was read, the people started to weep and mourn (8:9). They began to recognize that they had been violating God's law. Tears of conviction came to their eyes as they realized how they had transgressed the Lord's commands. The leaders were surprised by this show of emotion and encouraged the people to rejoice in God's blessings. This was to be a day of celebration for the completion of the wall!

Because of the people's response, a special day was then set aside for worship and remorse over sin. When that day arrived, the people mourned and read from the law, acknowledged their wrongs, and concluded with worship and a long prayer of confession (9:4-37). Even though Nehemiah isn't mentioned by name, as the governor, he and Ezra the priest were probably present and actively involved with the people on this "National Day of Prayer." Note these features of their corporate prayer:

- Sin was confessed. The people acknowledged past as well as present wrongs as they "stood and confessed their sins and the iniquities of their fathers" (verse 2).

- God's character was acknowledged. Worship of God formed the basis of their prayer as they made numerous references to God's goodness, His justice, and His mercy: "You are God, ready to pardon, gracious and merciful, slow to anger, abundant in kindness" (verse 17).[21]

- A solemn promise was given. To make sure their pledge

was not soon forgotten, the leaders—both spiritual and secular—signed a written document of their commitment: "We make a sure covenant and write it." And to put an explanation point to it, they said, "Our leaders, our Levites, and our priests seal it" (9:38).

A Lesson to Learn about Prayer

Confession is hard for us! That's because sin blinds us to God's standards. So we tend to resist God's tug on our hearts for as long as we can. Sometimes we hold on to our sin until it makes us ill, as happened with King David (Psalm 32:3-4), or until we die because of our stubborn rebellion (1 John 5:16). We tend to judge ourselves on the basis of those around us. We say, "I'm not as bad as that person!" In some cases, our conscience is "seared" so that we become numb to our iniquities (1 Timothy 4:2).

So what's the answer to our aversion to prayers of confession? We need to do as the people of Nehemiah's day did. We need to read God's Word in our Bibles. As we "understand the words of the Law" (Nehemiah 8:13) and are convicted by the Holy Spirit, then, like the Israelites, we will want to come before our holy God in worship and confession. That's what David did. When he finally gave in to God's conviction of his sin, he prayed, "I acknowledged my sin to You, and my iniquity I have not hidden. I said, 'I will confess my transgressions to the LORD,' and You forgave the iniquity of my sin" (Psalm 32:5).

Keep a short record with God. Stay in His Word. And constantly confess your sin. This will enable you to continually experience the joy of your salvation (Psalm 51:12).

Nehemiah prayed for remembrance—Nehemiah had finished his task—the wall was completed. In addition, social reforms were put into place and the city government was established. Nehemiah believed he had fulfilled the purpose given to him by God. So, in his last three prayers recorded in the Bible, this faithful servant asked God to...

"Remember me, O my God"...for protecting the house of God. "Do not wipe out my good deeds that I have done for the house of my God, and for its services!" (Nehemiah 13:14).

"Remember me, O my God"...for protecting the Sabbath (verses 15-22).

"Remember me, O my God"...for protecting the bloodline of Israel, by not allowing the people to marry pagans in violation of the Mosaic law (verses 29-31).

One scholar evaluates these prayers in this way: "With these words Nehemiah leaves the scene, committing himself and his discharge of duty to the Righteous Judge. His conscientious fidelity had brought him into collision not only with external enemies but with many of his own brethren....In these words he commits all to God."[22]

These three prayers from Nehemiah's heart were marvelously answered by the Lord. Today we have a permanent record of Nehemiah's memoirs—the book of Nehemiah—which provide us with a testimony of God's answers to his prayers.

A Lesson to Learn about Prayer

I know you and I agree on one thing—that we want our life to count for something. I would hate to come to the end of my life and have little to show for all my efforts, and I'm sure you feel the same way. Nehemiah felt this concern. His prayers of remembrance are a simple plea to God to please remember his faithfulness.

What are you asking God to remember about your life? What service have you performed for God's people? What ministry have you had to your family? Could you stand before God today and have Him say, "Well done, good and faithful servant" (Matthew 25:23)? If you feel that, so far, you have little to be remembered by, ask God to show you His purpose for your life. Then begin to fulfill that purpose with all your body, soul, and strength. You will then be able to pray, like Nehemiah, "Remember me, O my God, for good!" (Nehemiah 13:31).

Whether you are a man or woman, a husband or a wife, a single or a widow, you can learn much about prayer and purpose from the life of Nehemiah. His prayers teach us to:

- Pray to meet the needs of others. Nehemiah's awareness of

the condition of the people in Jerusalem moved him to pray and to seek and find a way to help them.

- Be open to God's purpose. Nehemiah caught a vision for God's purpose as he prayed, and it's probable that God will reveal His purpose for you as you pray.

- Commit to God's purpose. Nehemiah took a leave from his job, and you too may have to set aside certain activities so you can carry out God's plan for your life.

- Seek the support of others. Nehemiah could not complete God's purpose to build the wall alone...and you can't go it alone either!

- Persevere no matter what. Nehemiah faced multiple oppositions and pressed on, and to fulfill God's purpose you may have to do the same.

- Provide leadership through personal example. Nehemiah's blameless conduct shows us the makeup of a person God's people will follow to accomplish God's purposes. Follow in his steps!

Prayer Principles for You—Purpose

Prayer can be offered up anywhere and at any time.

Whether you (like Nehemiah) are standing before a king behind the great wall of a Persian palace or on the wall in Jerusalem, you can pray. Whether you are working on the job or in the kitchen or the garden, you can pray. You can pray all the time, in all the places your life takes you, and for all the people and concerns that make up your life. God is everywhere all the time, so you can pray anywhere at any time.

Prayer is to be a constant habit and attitude.

An attitude of God-consciousness leads to the habit of perpetual prayer. When God is never far from your mind, you will pray. When your every action or opposition is viewed as an opportunity to seek God's direction and trust in His protection, you will pray. Prayer will become automatic. It will become unceasing. It will become as natural as breathing. It will become a lifestyle. And, just as Nehemiah's prayers became a habit, yours will, too.

Prayer is not a substitute for action.

There is a balance we must seek between praying and acting, between faith in God and following God, between praying for God's will and doing God's will. Nehemiah prayed at every step of the way about what to do, and he also *did* something. He took action. Don't put off, in the name of prayer, what you know is right. Pray and then act. Sometimes an arrow prayer is all you can offer before proceeding ahead, and other times agonizing in prayer—perhaps for as long as 40 days and 40 nights—is required to prepare for action.

Prayer reveals your relationship with God.

God is not some distant deity. He is "our God," and, better yet, as Nehemiah often stated in his prayers, a very personal "my God." A close relationship with God does not come from a life filled with casual prayers offered up before meals. An intimate walk with God is not nurtured by rare utterances of prayer stated only in times of great need. No, fellowship with God is built on constant prayerfulness. The amount of time you spend praying reveals the measure of your closeness to God the Father. The practice of continual prayer gives you the assurance that God is standing beside you, is with you, through all of your days and through all of your difficulties. The more you pray, the better you will know God.

A Prayer for Purpose

God, You are the One who is and who may be known through Your self-revelation in the Scriptures. I lift grateful praise to You that I can say, along with Nehemiah, that You are "my God." I thank You that this revelation reached its fullness in Jesus Christ, Your Son and my Savior. Help me to develop the same level of passion for purpose that was in Nehemiah's heart. You gave him a mission, and he completed it. As You reveal Your will for me—each mission that you ask of me—I pray that I will embrace it. May I trust You in Your purposes, and finish the work You give me to do. And when I falter, encourage me. "Remember me, O my God...and spare me according to the greatness of Your mercy!...Remember me, O my God, for good!" Amen.[23]

7

Prayers to Grow in Character

You asked, "Who is this that hides counsel without knowledge?" Therefore I have uttered what I did not understand, things too wonderful for me, which I did not know...Therefore I abhor myself, and repent in dust and ashes

—JOB 42:3,6

When Bad Things Happen to Good People is the title of a best-selling book published more than 35 years ago. It was written by Rabbi Harold Kushner after he lost his son to a rare aging disease. Like many who have faced some kind of tragedy or another, Rabbi Kushner asked the question, "If God exists and He is supposed to be loving and kind, how could He do this to me and to my innocent child?"

Rabbi Kushner's question about the suffering of the "innocent" is one that has been asked by others all through the centuries. Although many of these observations have been lost to us, I'm quite sure some of these same individuals posed the same question of fairness.

But one noteworthy ancient account of suffering and how to successfully handle "bad things" has been preserved for us in the Bible—the story of a man named Job. His story details the testing and refining process he endured in the midst of suffering.

Character Forged in Suffering

As we continue learning about how we can know God through prayer and surveying the prayers of those who knew him well, it's important to understand that the books of the Bible are not in chronological order. The book of Job, which contains the life and prayers of Job, appears near the middle of the Bible. It is, however, thought by Bible scholars to be the oldest of all the biblical records. Job probably lived around the time of Abraham.

Who was Job? The Bible says he was a man of great wealth and influence. He is described as "the greatest of all the people of the East" (Job 1:3). Besides great fortune, he had a wife and ten children. Job was so abundantly blessed that it seemed as if God had "made a hedge around him" (verse 10).

But things changed. Within the space of a few hours, Job went from riches to rags. He lost everything—all his children, all his wealth, and even his health. How would he respond to such devastation? Satan, the accuser of the brethren (Revelation 12:10), suggested to God that Job "will surely curse You to Your face!" (Job 1:11; 2:5). Even Job's wife advised him to "curse

God and die!" (2:9). Yet despite such great tragedy and his wife's discouraging words, the Bible tells us, "In all this Job did not sin with his lips" (verse 10). He held fast to his integrity (verse 9).

"Character" has been described as what you are when you are alone. This was truly Job's situation. Alone, penniless, and covered from head to foot with painful boils, we see his inner character revealed through his prayers.

Prayer in the Life of Job

The Bible testifies that Job "was blameless and upright, and one who feared God and shunned evil" (1:1). Surely with what you would witness from reading just the first three chapters of this man's life story—the details of his pain and suffering—you would expect to read about doubt, anger, and bewilderment. But not so with Job. God reports Job "did not sin with his lips" (2:10). And so the realization begins to sink in: It would be very difficult for Job to possess such sterling character without being a man of prayer. And a man of prayer he was!

Job prayed a prayer of intercession—Prayer gives us a unique privilege: We can intercede for others. Job's own story begins with prayer for his children (1:4-5) and ends with prayer for his friends (42:10). Job's intercession for his family is somewhat unique in Scripture, and is seen practiced only in a few instances:

- Rebekah was barren, and "Isaac pleaded with the LORD for his wife, because she was barren" (Genesis 25:21).

- Miriam, Moses' sister, was punished with leprosy because she questioned his leadership, and "Moses cried out to the Lord, saying, 'Please heal her, O God, I pray!'" (Numbers 12:13).

- King David's newborn child was sick, and "David therefore pleaded with God for the child, and David fasted and went in and lay all night on the ground" (2 Samuel 12:16).

- A child possessed with an evil spirit was brought to Jesus and the father asked Jesus, "If You can do anything, have compassion on us and help us" (Mark 9:22).

Job, too, was a concerned parent. He prayed faithfully for his seven sons and three daughters, a further indicator of the depth of his character and spiritual devotion. What an example Job sets for parents! "He would rise early in the morning and offer burnt offerings according to the number of them all. For Job said, 'It may be that my sons have sinned and cursed God in their hearts.' Thus Job did regularly" (Job 1:5).

Over the years, I've tried to follow Job's example and pray regularly for my two daughters. When they were young, I prayed for God to work in their hearts, that they would come to know Jesus as their salvation. As they grew into their teen years, I prayed for God to bring godly young men into their lives. And now I pray for their husbands, homes, children, and their continued commitment to God. Praying for grandchildren is a new dimension to my prayers. Let me say from my heart, if you are a parent or grandparent, don't neglect to pray for your children and your children's children!

This practice could actually become a full-time job, as my wife,

Elizabeth, learned one day while she was speaking at a women's conference. During one of the breaks, a woman shared that she had committed to praying ten minutes a day for her first grandchild when it arrived. (What an admirable commitment!) Now the faithful grandmother has 23 grandchildren and has faithfully kept her daily appointment to pray for each grandchild for ten minutes every day. That adds up to about four hours of prayer each day!

A Lesson to Learn about Prayer

Prayer is a heart exercise. It's an act of communicating with the Eternal about what's most important and pressing in your life. As for Job, his *focus* was on what was most important and pressing—his family and their spiritual condition. What's important and pressing in your life? Is your focus on those closest to you—your family members?

Along with a focus on family should come *frequency.* Job prayed "regularly." Are you praying regularly for those closest to you? For others? In intercession?

But Job's prayer life teaches us more. In addition to focus and frequency there should be a *fervency.* Job "would rise early in the morning and offer burnt offerings," not just one offering, but "burnt offerings according to the number of them all"—all ten of his children (1:5). James 5:16 is true: "The effective, fervent prayer of a righteous man avails much." May we learn the lessons of intercessory prayer well: Pray with focus, with frequency, and with fervency!

Job prayed a prayer of resignation—The loss of all your possessions would pale next to the loss of all your children. That would be a tragedy beyond belief! How would you respond to a tragedy of this magnitude? How *could* you?

Job continues to be an excellent model to follow. He expressed all the Old Testament elements of grief as he "arose, tore his robe, and shaved his head." But he also took the all-important next step: "He fell to the ground and worshiped." Instead of cursing God as some do when struck with tragedy, Job offered up a prayer of trust, blessing the name of God (Job 1:20-21).

Job's prayer of resignation to the providential hand of God was, "The LORD gave, and the LORD has taken away" (verse 21). His godly response certainly disproved Satan's accusations that, if God allowed Satan to afflict Job, Job would curse God (1:11; 2:5). Instead, Job trusted in God and blessed His name.

Job understood something of the nature and attributes of God. His prayer of resignation was simply an act of honoring God for His providence and direction. In spite of how circumstances looked on the surface, the sovereign God of the universe was working out His will. Therefore, everything would be all right for Job.

A Lesson to Learn about Prayer

When Job's wife suggested that he curse God and die, Job answered her in a way that communicated his resignation to God's will: "Shall we indeed accept good from God, and shall we not accept adversity?" (2:10). Sometimes when we're suffering, if we're not careful, we can act like Job's wife and say foolish things about God and our situation. Prayer helps us submit to what God is doing in our lives in a God-honoring way.

Remember two things as you pray: First, everything that happens to you passes through God—even what seems like tragedy (1:6–2:10). And second, all God takes you through is for your ultimate good and His glory. God seeks to give only "good things" to His children (Matthew 7:11).

The next time tragedy strikes and you are at a loss for reasons why, let Jesus' prayer of resignation to God the Father right before Jesus' crucifixion be your prayer: "Not as I will, but as You will" (Matthew 26:39).

Job prayed a prayer of self-pity—With great resolve and trust, Job began his ordeal of suffering. But after experiencing his pain and suffering for a week (Job 2:11-13), Job was ready to give up, to be freed from his discomfort, and to die. Unfortunately, he moaned forth a prayer of self-pity: "Oh, that I might have my request, that God would grant me the thing that I long for! That it would please God to crush me, that He would loose His hand and cut me off!" (6:8).

This is one prayer request God was not going to grant to Job. God had a greater plan for His servant, and death at this time was not an option. Job's mettle was being tested in the fire of adversity to see if his was truly a pure faith, a faith that is more precious than gold (1 Peter 1:7).

A Lesson to Learn about Prayer

Our tendency, like Job's, is to want to give up and get out of any "bad things" going on in our life...fast! We have no problem trusting God in the good times, but to trust Him during the difficult times definitely stretches our faith. But this is exactly where God wants us and what He wants of us: He wants us to depend on Him completely. God says, "My grace is sufficient for you, for My strength is made perfect in weakness" (2 Corinthians 12:9).

The next time you feel like giving up, remember God's grace. It will see you through your trial. And rather than praying for God to "end it all," pray that God would "use it all" for His glory and your good.

Job prayed a prayer for understanding—In the midst of his horrendous suffering, some of Job's friends came to comfort him. (As you'll see, with friends like these, Job didn't need enemies!) An incorrect theology caused them to conclude that Job was suffering because of some personal sin. Furthermore, they were all—including Job—unaware of the discussion that had taken place earlier between God and Satan (Job 1:6–2:7).

The dialogue between Job and his friends continues back and forth throughout most of the book of Job (3:1 to 37:24). When Bildad accused Job of sin, Job denied doing wrong and prayed to God in an almost daring way, asking for answers. Job said, "I will say to God, 'Do not condemn me; Show me why You contend with me'" (10:2).

Prayers for understanding are acceptable. Did not Mary, a virgin, ask, "How can this be?" (Luke 1:34) when told the news that she would conceive and give birth to the Son of God? The angel Gabriel never rebuked Mary's questioning. Rather, he patiently told her how the miraculous event would take place (verse 35).

But poor Job, in his efforts to understand how and why his suffering was taking place, tried to take God to task. He felt he was being unjustly accused and demanded that God, the Judge, show him proof of his condemnation. In a terrible moment, overwhelmed by physical pain and emotional sorrow, Job uttered the shameless thought that God had created him only to destroy him. Throughout this prayer, delivered in agony and suffering, Job did not once mention the name of God. He prayed for understanding, but sought his own answers while continuing to maintain his innocence before God (Job 10:2-22).

A Lesson to Learn about Prayer

Job lived to regret many of the statements he made to God in this prayer and others. But at this time in his suffering, and in his frustration to understand what was happening, Job got caught up in demanding answers, misrepresenting God, and forgetting about God's love and concern for him.

Are you presently suffering in some area of your life? Examine your prayers to see if perhaps you are doing as Job did by demanding answers. In your desperation to understand what is happening, resist the urge to "take

God to task." Don't ask "Why?" as Job did. Rather, follow Mary's example and humbly ask, "How?" Don't pray to understand. Pray instead for a better understanding of God. And continue to put your trust in the Righteous Judge.

Job prayed a prayer of supplication—To pray in supplication means to ask earnestly, to entreat, to plead, or to implore. In the midst of his personal pain and the incessant badgering of his friends, Job continued to ask for an opportunity to declare his innocence before God. He wanted a chance to plead his case before the Almighty Judge. Job prayed, "Oh, that I...might come to His seat! I would present my case before Him" (23:3-4).

A Lesson to Learn about Prayer

Pain and suffering are hard to endure. So we plead. We entreat. We implore. We want to be cured, to be happy, to have justice served. Then, if the suffering continues and the pain doesn't go away, or our situation doesn't improve, we can easily become impatient. All these concerns are valid, but ultimately we must ask: Whose purposes are served if our prayers for relief are answered? Maybe others', but mostly our own.

It's good to learn to plead your case before the Righteous Judge through prayer, in supplication. But you must also learn to let God, the Judge, determine who is best served by your situation. Thank God for His love and for His wonderful plan for your life. "I know the thoughts that I think toward you, says the LORD, thoughts of peace and not of evil, to give you a future and a hope" (Jeremiah 29:11).

Job prayed a prayer of repentance—From a simple-but-profound prayer of trust—"The LORD gave, and the LORD has taken away; blessed be the name of the LORD" (Job 1:21)—Job began to spiral down through a series of prayers of complaint and harsh questioning. Eventually, God had enough. Speaking to Job out of a whirlwind, God interrogated Job and rebuked his inability to truly understand Him and trust in His wisdom (38:1–41:34).

At the end of God's inquisition, Job returned to his previous simple trust in God. Yet now it was a trust built on better understanding. In confession and repentance, Job humbly acknowledged God's greatness and his own insolence. He submissively accepted his situation and relinquished his desire to know why. Hear his repentance: "I have uttered what I did not understand, things too wonderful for me, which I did not know...I abhor myself, and repent in dust and ashes" (42:3,6).

Note that nothing had changed for Job. He was still covered with boils. He was still without possessions and family. God hadn't changed a thing...but He had transformed the heart of his servant Job, and that's what God's top priority was for Job. Job became a *humble* servant of God—one who accepted God's will without complaints, questions, or ignorance! (And, as a footnote, "the

LORD blessed the latter days of Job more than his beginning." He gave Job seven more sons and three more daughters, and health to live to 140 years old and see "his children and grandchildren for four generations"—42:12-16.)

A Lesson to Learn about Prayer

Have you ever made an inappropriate statement to or about another person simply because you didn't have all the facts? Unfortunately, we are often guilty of praying inappropriately to and about God, because we are ignorant of the facts about God and His will.

Be sure and read God's rebuke of Job's ignorance for yourself (38:1–41:34). Then pray your own prayer of repentance for any ignoble thoughts you've had about God or are having now. Thank Him for His majesty and power. Thank Him for His sovereignty in your life. Whatever you do, don't question the wisdom of God. Remember, He doesn't answer to you. You answer to Him!

The book of Job and the man Job give us an insightful look at interaction between God and Satan. They give us a sobering look at how we can misjudge the suffering of others. They give us a humbling look at how we wrongly approach our mighty and magnificent God. And they give us a privileged look into the celestial realm of God and His control over all things.

In the end, when God finally spoke to Job, He didn't give Job an answer to his "why" question. Instead, God impressed upon Job that it was better to know God than to know answers. Job's suffering was a test to affirm and refine his character...and another opportunity for God to glorify Himself. This puts a fresh spin on our suffering, doesn't it? Who wouldn't want their character honed and their God honored?

Prayer Principles for You—Character

Prayer helps you better understand the mind of God.

Surely you've had times when you've been mad or upset because something negative happened in your life. You wanted to take your frustrations out on someone, and you ended up taking them out on God. "Why, God?" you asked. "Why me? What did I do?"

At times like these, coming before your heavenly Father in prayer and asking Him for answers, direction, and wisdom leads to a better understanding of His will for your life. You may not always see the reasons for your suffering or why it is necessary, but hopefully you see the results. In Job, one result was a more humble heart. What is God wanting to transform in your life, and how are you responding to His loving hand?

Prayer stimulates self-examination.

In times of torment, rather than ask, "God, *why* are You doing this to me?" remember to pray, "Lord, *what* are You doing to me? What are You teaching me as I suffer? Is there something You want from me?" Honestly examining your life through prayer allows you to join with God's purposes for your spiritual perfection (James 1:4). Suffering tests your character, and you should welcome God's process for character-building. Job prayed consistently during his time of intense suffering and was a better man afterward.

You are called to purify your heart (James 4:8), so examine yourself. And invite divine scrutiny as well. Open your heart to God and pray, "Examine me, O LORD, and prove me; try my mind and my heart" (Psalm 26:2). God says the end result of suffering tempered by prayer will be a genuine faith which, though "tested by fire, may be found to praise, honor, and glory at the revelation of Jesus Christ" (1 Peter 1:7).

Prayer refocuses your perspective.

What can you do when your life caves in? Rather than question or curse, pray. As sure as lifting your gaze upward refocuses your sight, lifting prayers upward to God refocuses your perspective. The act of prayer involves God in your situation, your suffering. When the roof caved in (figuratively and literally) on Job's life, Job immediately went to God in prayer and worshiped. He knew the right place to focus—on God!

Prayer restores relationships.

Have you discovered that you cannot be angry at someone and pray for him or her at the same time? That's because prayer requires a loving, caring heart. When Job's friends heard about his misfortune, they came to criticize him. Yet Job prayed for his friends (Job 42:8-10).

Everyone has problem relationships and difficult people to deal with. For some, it's a person at work, or a boss. For others, it's a person right under their own roof.

And for still others, it's a person from the past. God's solution in every instance is prayer.

Are you praying for those who have hurt you? Have you forgiven them? It's never easy! But following the teaching of Jesus is the first step to restoring relationships. He said, "Pray for those who spitefully use you" (Luke 6:28). Also important is following the example of Jesus— He prayed for those who crucified him: "Father, forgive them, for they do not know what they do" (Luke 23:34).

A Prayer for Character

God, it was Job who cried out, "I know that my Redeemer lives, and He shall stand at last on the earth." As person after person challenged his character, Job showed the best defense when criticism runs high: It is to know in my heart that "my Redeemer lives," and that He will vindicate me.

You, O Lord, are sovereign. You know everything that happens to me—including that which is unjust. And You know Your purpose in my suffering. Weave in me the kind of strong moral and spiritual character exhibited by Job. Keep me on the path of righteousness. Help me remember that, because I know You, I don't have to understand why You allow me to experience the things that come my way. It is enough to know that You will care for me. Amen.[24]

8

Prayers to Grow in Determination

Through the LORD's mercies we are not consumed, because His compassions fail not. They are new every morning; great is Your faithfulness. "The LORD is my portion," says my soul, Therefore I hope in Him!"

—LAMENTATIONS 3:22-24

Determination is defined as firmness of purpose, a resoluteness of heart. It's also what helps a man or woman endure overwhelming odds in order to achieve incredible feats. It's the kind of resolve that has characterized the life and ministry of Joni Eareckson Tada.

Joni became paralyzed from the neck down in a diving

accident when she was just a teen girl. You can read the story of her struggles with acceptance, adjustment, and rehabilitation in her now-classic book, *Joni*.[25] Once Joni settled things with God, she determined to use her "accident" as an opportunity to serve God. But how could she be useful to God? She was a quadriplegic. The nerves from her brain to the rest of her body had been permanently damaged. She was unable to use her arms or legs.

This is where God's grace and Joni's determination—her resoluteness of heart—came in for Joni. With great resolve, Joni has since trained both her mind and her body to serve the Lord. When you read her books or listen to her speak today, you are immediately aware of the depth of her spiritual maturity and impressed with her ability to speak totally from memory, quoting numerous passages of Scripture.

But for Joni, determination didn't stop with the spiritual aspect, as essential as that is. With great difficulty and years of physical therapy, Joni has gained the ability to perform many everyday physical tasks. She has also developed some limited use of her arms and can direct her own wheelchair. Amazingly, Joni can even drive a specially equipped van.

Today, Joni and her husband, Ken, travel throughout the world distributing wheelchairs to the needy, preaching the love of Jesus Christ, and sharing hope with the disabled and their loved ones. Joni's determination helped turn tragedy into a triumph which has been, and I hope will continue to be, an inspiration to countless millions.

Joni's story is truly motivating. What she has accomplished with limited physical abilities should prompt you and me to evaluate our own lives and see what we might accomplish if we were more determined.

Firmness of Purpose

Our list of people who knew God well through prayer is continuing to expand. With each new addition, we are coming to see more and more the transforming power of prayer and the unique qualities prayer can energize within us.

In this chapter we will look at Jeremiah and his prayers.

Jeremiah was a prophet in the Old Testament who was told by God early in his ministry that his preaching would be rejected by the people of Israel (Jeremiah 7:27-29). Undaunted, Jeremiah continued to fulfill God's purpose for his life and his ministry. He preached forth God's message for portions of five decades, boldly confronting the last five kings of Israel and their spiritually rebellious people. And, in spite of death threats, physical deprivation, humiliation, and resistance to his message, Jeremiah preached for 40 years. Now that's firmness of purpose!

At this point, I have to stop and make a confession. Jeremiah was not on my initial list of people whose prayers I wanted to study and share with you. The book of Jeremiah can get lost between the grandeur of Isaiah and the fascinating prophecies of Ezekiel and Daniel. Jeremiah, the man, also doesn't stand out like many of the other great prayer personalities of the Old Testament—men like Abraham, Moses, and Daniel, or women like Hannah and Mary.

All of these more familiar and thrilling people of prayer appeared, on the surface, to be more exciting to study than a man who has been labeled by many as "the weeping prophet." His prayers are stained with tears of anguish because of the spiritual rebellion of both the leaders and the people and because of the coming invasion by the Babylonian army.

But, I hope that as we take a closer look at this remarkable man, like me, you will discover in Jeremiah a person who uttered emotional and heartfelt prayers filled with practical lessons. Jeremiah saw his nation in rebellion against God and was angered by their sinfulness, but his heart grieved with compassion for the people as he anticipated the misery of their prophesied captivity.

Prayer in the Life of Jeremiah

Many of Jeremiah's prayers were prompted by the treachery and cruelty of his own people. Others were simply prayers of sincere sympathy. One commentator gave this tribute to Jeremiah and his prayers: "Jeremiah's temperament, his tragic experiences, his sensitive religious nature, all combine to inspire his prayers with a passion and familiarity which have no parallel anywhere."[26]

Jeremiah's prayer of inability—As we begin reading Jeremiah's autobiography, immediately we are impressed with his honesty. Not many people, including me, would want the public to read their very first prayer in response to God's call on their lives, especially if they used their inexperience and age as excuses for not wanting to serve God. Jeremiah prayed, "Ah, Lord GOD! Behold, I cannot speak, for I am a youth" (Jeremiah 1:6).

Yet as we saw with Moses, God—the one calling Jeremiah—was ready, willing, and able to stand with him and empower him to fulfill the calling. God gave Jeremiah this reassurance: "Do not be afraid...for I am with you to deliver you....Behold, I have put My words in your mouth" (verses 8-9).

Resting completely in the Lord, Jeremiah accepted God's call.

From that point onward, he lived out that calling by going out to challenge a sinful nation of worldly leaders, false prophets, and others who wanted to kill him.[27]

A Lesson to Learn about Prayer

In his first recorded prayer, Jeremiah teaches us a significant lesson: God knows your heart. He knows your concerns and fears. So, like Jeremiah, you can be honest with God. Jeremiah didn't believe he was the man for the job... and he said so. He was young, probably 20 to 25 years old. He also pointed out to God that he had very little experience. He was just an average guy from a small town.

Can you identify? Is God asking something of you? And are you hesitating because of what you perceive as limitations? Are you fearful like Jeremiah? Express your fears. Open your heart to God. Then, like Jeremiah, put your trust in God to go before you, calm your fears, and use His transforming power to turn your limitations into unlimited possibilities.

Jeremiah's prayer of concern—The prevailing hope of the Israelites in Jeremiah's day was that God would bring peace to their land. These hopes had been offered up by the priests and false prophets (6:13; 14:14). But God gave an entirely different picture of what was to come (2:1–4:9). Like many other prophets in the Old Testament, Jeremiah was horrified at God's prophetic words of judgment. In his confusion, Jeremiah asked God, "Is it peace or the sword?" (see 4:10).

Upon hearing the bad news, Jeremiah's heart went out to the people: "O my soul, my soul! I am pained in my very heart!" (verse 19).

A Lesson to Learn about Prayer

As a prophet, Jeremiah understood what God was about to do to His people, and he was deeply concerned. His heart ached for the coming judgment. Centuries later, the apostle Paul, too, was pained for his fellow Jews and was willing (if it were possible) to exchange his own soul for the salvation of his countrymen (Romans 9:1-3).

What prayer concerns are on your heart? Your family's well-being? Your stock portfolio? Your health? Your social position? Or do your prayer interests center on the salvation of your lost friends and relatives? The return of a wayward child? The repentance of a sinning and hardened brother or sister?

Take a prayer lesson from Jeremiah. Develop a greater sensitivity for the condition of the lost and wayward. How can you do this? By faithfully praying for them. Praying will fill your heart with compassion.

Jeremiah was told not to pray—Amazingly, three times, God told His spokesman Jeremiah *not* to pray.[28] This must have been hard for Jeremiah. He had great concern for God's people. But each time God gave this unusual command, there was a reason for it—the people had slid further into rebellion. They were sinking deeper and deeper into sin, and their fate as an idolatrous nation was being sealed. They chose not to listen. Therefore, in judgment, they would not be able to listen.

A Lesson to Learn about Prayer

God commanded Jeremiah not to pray. This was a divine decree. The people were unwilling to repent and flagrantly continued in their idol worship. Thus there was no longer any hope for them.

But, praying brother or sister, God has given you and me no such command. Look around you. What do you see? Men and women flagrant in their sin? People who seem to be resistant to the gospel? What is your tendency? You may find yourself wanting to give up on them. You may even stop praying for them. But these people are actually prayer opportunities, prayer projects.

God is not asking you to give up on anyone. He is not asking you to stop praying for the salvation of even the most vile of sinners. You don't know how God plans to work in each life, so pray faithfully for those who need the Savior. Never give up! Only God knows who will respond to the Spirit's call.

Jeremiah prayed for direction—The people and their leaders had persistently refused to allow God to give them direction. Therefore, judgment was coming (Jeremiah 10:17-22).

By contrast, Jeremiah listened to God. His prayer for direction was in response to another round of God's judgments. In this prayer, Jeremiah shifted from concern for the people to his own need for direction from God. The people had already rejected God's offer. But Jeremiah understood that man is incapable of directing his own steps (verse 23). So he asked God to correct him and guide him in the right direction. He pleaded with God and prayed, "Correct me, but with justice; not in Your anger, lest You bring me to nothing" (verse 24).

A Lesson to Learn about Prayer

Don't be afraid to pray for God to do whatever is necessary to correct you. Jeremiah understood the power and judgment of God and he wanted no part of God's crushing judgment. His desire was that God would correct him with merciful and loving justice if and when he veered off the path.

God will give you direction if you ask for it. And His loving correction is better than the consequences of living outside the will of God. So pray and "trust in the LORD... lean not on your own understanding; in all your ways acknowledge Him," is the advice of Proverbs 3:5-6...if you want God to "direct your paths."

Jeremiah prayed for justice—To Jeremiah's surprise, the people of his hometown were plotting to kill him (Jeremiah 11:18-23). They were angered by his repeated predictions of doom. What did Jeremiah do? He prayed. He asked God to judge righteously and bring justice to their murderous hearts (verse 20).

God responded to Jeremiah's prayer with, "Behold, I will punish them" (verse 22).

Encouraged by God's answer, Jeremiah again prayed for justice, but this time he broadened his prayer by asking the question many of us have often asked: "Why does the way of the wicked prosper?" (12:1). Jeremiah was aware of the righteousness and justice of God. He knew that ultimately, God's justice would prevail. But he was impatient. He wanted justice—now!

God's prophet and the nation of Israel were in extreme difficulty. Frustrated, Jeremiah wanted things to return to normal. He blamed the wicked for contributing to his perilous situation and the desperate condition of the land. He wanted God to deal with them.

A Lesson to Learn about Prayer

It's only natural for us to want fair play—justice for those who take advantage of others. Like Jeremiah, you may want the wicked to get what they deserve. And you've prayed for God to move quickly (more accurately, to move according to *your* timetable)! But as with Jeremiah, God doesn't always respond as quickly as we would like. In fact, it sometimes seems as if He might never respond.

But we know that God does ultimately respond. The righteous will be vindicated, and the wicked will be judged. That's the way it is with God.

The next time you are tempted to pray for justice, remember first how much trouble you would be in if you were given what you truly deserve. Thank God for His mercy given to you through Jesus Christ. Then plead for God's mercy for the wicked while there is time for them to repent. The time is most surely coming when God's mercy will turn to wrath.

Jeremiah prayed for relief—Within Jeremiah's prayer for justice, we see the prophet contrasting himself with the wicked. Jeremiah, in essence, prayed, "God, You know me. You know my heart. You know I'm not like these people who talk about You with their mouth but have You far from their mind" (see 12:2). The prophet asked God, in the language of our day, "God, could you cut me a little slack?" He called on God for relief.

God did not respond to Jeremiah's question about the wicked. But He did respond to Jeremiah's hint for relief from persecution by giving him a challenge. In effect, God said, "If you think what you are experiencing is bad, and you feel like turning in your prophet's badge, what will you do when the battle gets even harder? You run with the men of your town, the 'footmen,' and you are weary. How will you contend with the king, his leaders, the priests, and the 'horses'?" (see verse 5).[29]

A Lesson to Learn about Prayer

If you have ever experienced the loss of a loved one or are facing a serious illness, you know that God's answers to your prayers are not always what you want or expect. Sometimes His answers are hard to understand. You pray for relief, but instead, things get worse.

Should negative developments change your commitment to pray and to keep asking of God? No. God does not promise to keep you from the difficulties of life. But He does promise to sustain you through them. So, even though the going gets tough and there seems to be no relief in sight, you can praise God along with David: "Yea, though I walk through the valley of the shadow of death, I will fear no evil; for You are with me" (Psalm 23:4).

Jeremiah prayed in doubt—While Jeremiah was in prison and Jerusalem was under siege, God told Jeremiah to buy a field in his hometown (Jeremiah 32:1-15). Afterward, Jeremiah had "buyer's remorse." This had to be the worst land deal ever! Jeremiah wondered, *Did I do the right thing? Did I misunderstand God's directions?* The enemy was ready to storm the walls, and the city was about to be destroyed. Jeremiah couldn't understand why God had him purchase the field at *this* time. He doubted if he had done the right thing. So Jeremiah took his doubts to the Lord in prayer.

Doubt is not sin. But it can lead to sin if it erodes our trust in God. Doubt gave Jeremiah a restless and unsettled state of mind. But Jeremiah had the right response. He prayed and took his misgivings to God. And God answered with reassurance. What Jeremiah had done was right, even if he couldn't understand the reason for it. God answered with, "Is there anything too hard for Me?" (verse 27). God went on to say that one day the land would again be inhabited and the fields would again produce crops (verses 42-44). Jeremiah's faith could be restored in his own obedience and his trust in God's promise to restore the people to the land.

A Lesson to Learn about Prayer

A mind that wavers is a mind that is not completely convinced that God's way is best. Doubt treats God's Word like human advice. Doubt allows one to retain the option to disobey. But we should see doubt as a reminder of our need to pray.

Ask God to dispel your fears and concerns. And honestly ask yourself why you are doubting. Is it because you don't believe you can trust God? Or is it because you don't want to trust God? When you doubt, remember, there isn't anything too hard for God.

In the world's eyes, Jeremiah was a failure. He was rejected by his neighbors, his family, the religious leaders of his day, his friends, the masses of people, and four of the five kings who heard his message.[30] But in God's eyes, Jeremiah was one of the most successful people in all history. "How is that?" you ask.

Success, in God's eyes, means obedience and faithfulness. Regardless of the cost, Jeremiah was determined to fulfill God's calling on his life. Do you want to be successful in God's eyes? Then with the strength that only God can provide, resolve to fight the good fight of faith, to finish the race, to keep the faith—at whatever the cost.

Prayer Principles for You—Determination

Prayer is your response to God's working.

God is constantly at work in history, in your life, and in the lives of those around you. Seeing how God is working in the world should have a profound spiritual effect on you. Like Jeremiah, it should move you to pray.

What sort of spiritual response are you making to the events in your life? Do you view them as chance? Luck? With indifference? Or do you view these events as God at work? Through prayer, choose to enter what God is doing and become a partner with Him.

Prayer strengthens your relationship with God.

Your relationship with God is your most important relationship, bar none. But to nurture that relationship requires you to spend time with Him in prayer and His Word. Jeremiah spent 40 years battling the spiritual apathy of the Israelites. He was hated and ostracized, but he was never alone. He had a close and comforting relationship with God. It was this priceless closeness and companionship that pulled him through an incredibly difficult life.

Are you feeling alone or misunderstood by family or friends because of your beliefs? You are not alone. God is ever present. Why not spend time strengthening your relationship with Him in prayer today? At times, this relationship may be all you have. But it will be all you need!

Prayer does not guarantee a positive answer.

Just because you pray doesn't mean you will get what you are praying for. Prayer in and of itself doesn't have any guarantees. It isn't a magic wand you can wave to receive your every wish.

Whatever is happening in your life, you have the great privilege of praying to the creator and sustainer of life. It is God's job to answer according to His will. And there are certain truths you can know for sure: God has promised to supply all your needs (Philippians 4:19), He has promised His presence (Joshua 1:9), and He has promised His guidance and His strength (Proverbs 3:5-6; Philippians 4:13).

Jeremiah prayed for revival, deliverance, and relief—all good things. But none of these requests were answered in the affirmative. God had other plans: He was disciplining His children. God would bring about revival, deliverance, and relief, but not in Jeremiah's lifetime. Nevertheless, Jeremiah prayed...and so must you, even if you don't see positive results.

Prayer allows you to reveal your deepest thoughts.

When you come into the presence of a holy God, your thoughts should not center on withholding anything, but on exposing your life to God's all-seeing eyes. Jeremiah acknowledged God's ability to look into his heart. "You, O LORD, know me; You have seen me, and You have tested my heart toward You" (Jeremiah 12:3). Therefore, Jeremiah could be honest with God about his feelings. He was overcome with grief on several occasions because of what was about to happen to the nation of Israel. His feelings began to get the best of him and he became depressed and disheartened.

Be honest with God. Express your feelings. Open yourself up to His care. And, like Jeremiah, be ready to receive God's encouragement. But also, again like Jeremiah, be ready to receive God's reprimand and correction if your attitude needs to change (10:23-24).

Prayer fosters spiritual revival.

Every great revival in the history of the church began with prayer. One instance was in the upper room when the disciples prayed, the Spirit came, and the disciples went out and preached boldly about the risen Savior. Another example is the great student movements of the nineteenth century, when college students prayed and the Spirit empowered hundreds of them to go to the ends of the earth and proclaim Jesus Christ.

Friend, prayer is the common denominator in revival. When it comes to your own personal revival, prayer opens your heart to the Spirit's transforming power in your life. Jeremiah was downcast and defeated on many occasions. But on those times when he was at his lowest, he prayed, and God energized his soul and transformed his timid heart into a heart of fiery determination.

Prayer strengthens your determination.

It's easy to become discouraged, isn't it? Everyone

tells you what can't be done. That you don't have the education, the physical or mental abilities. It seems like no one is there to encourage you...or so you think. But God is there. And in prayer you can "be of good courage," knowing "He shall strengthen your heart" (Psalm 31:24).

It is in your times of discouragement that prayer helps rekindle your desires and motivation. You once again see things from God's perspective. In prayer your determination is strengthened and your resolve stiffened as you answer God's question to Jeremiah, "Is there anything too hard for Me?" And in the strength and power of the Holy Spirit, you get up off your knees. With renewed confidence, you again enter into the struggles that just a few minutes before were more than you could handle. Now that's the transforming power of prayer!

A Prayer for Determination

Lord God, who made heaven and earth and to whom nothing is too difficult, I thank You for the example of determination found in the life of Your faithful prophet Jeremiah. May I follow his example and look to You for the strength I need to continue on whenever I am misunderstood, slandered, or persecuted. May I boldly proclaim Your Word with the same determination Jeremiah had, keeping in mind his words of hope that Your mercy and compassion are new every morning—great is Your faithfulness! Amen.[31]

9

Prayers to Grow in Integrity

Daniel...knelt down on his knees three times that day,
and prayed and gave thanks before his God,
as was his custom since early days.

—Daniel 6:10

Recently I was a guest in a pastor's home. As we visited, I couldn't help but notice one massive floor-to-ceiling bookcase in his living room dedicated to books about the Civil War. A great many of those books were about the "Gray Fox," Robert E. Lee. Being a bit of a Civil War buff myself, I asked the pastor if he had read a certain book about Lee on leadership ability. He immediately pointed me to the book prominently displayed on one of the shelves. He shared how much he enjoyed speaking to groups of men about "Lee, the Christian."

Like so many who read and write about the life of this unique individual, the consensus is always that Robert E. Lee was a man of integrity. Even before the Southern states formally withdrew from the Union, Lee's character and military abilities were so well-known and admired that President Lincoln asked him to assume command of the Union Army. Lee, however, refused the president's offer and led the men of the South well, almost winning the war with his military strategies. When the battlefield smoke finally cleared at the end of the fighting, one man had won the deep respect and admiration of the leaders and men on both sides of the conflict. That man was Robert E. Lee.

Living a Life of Integrity

The Old Testament prophet and statesman, Daniel, also lived a life of integrity. And that's saying a lot. Why? Because Daniel lived a long time. He lived and served from the reign of King Jehoiakim in Judah through the 70 years of the captivity of God's people by the Babylonians, and into the reigns of Cyrus and Darius, two rulers of the Medo-Persian Empire. So Daniel's service to God lasted a span of more than 80 years. And through all those years, and through every one of those pagan societies, Daniel consistently exhibited a life of integrity.

In the Bible, we see Daniel's integrity affirmed on three different occasions and from three sources.

The first source was his enemies—"The governors and satraps sought to find some charge against Daniel concerning the kingdom; but they could find no charge or fault, because he was faithful; nor was there any error or fault found in him" (Daniel 6:4).

The second source was heavenly messengers—In one of the prophetic visions Daniel received, the mighty Gabriel said to Daniel, "You are greatly beloved" (9:23). Then in another vision, another angel twice addressed him as, "O Daniel, man greatly beloved" (10:11,19).

The third source was God Himself as He spoke through the prophet Ezekiel—God was pronouncing judgment on His unfaithful people and gave this testimonial of Daniel's character: "Even if these three men, Noah, Daniel, and Job, were in [the land of Israel], they would deliver only themselves by their righteousness" (Ezekiel 14:14).

This was an amazing confirmation as God singled out Daniel to stand alongside the likes of Noah and Job. And it was especially significant coming through Ezekiel. Why? Because Ezekiel was a contemporary who lived in the same country as Daniel. He was a fellow-exile at the same time as Daniel, and would have known of Daniel's character because Daniel was a public figure.

So, how was living a life of integrity possible some 2500 years ago in the midst of spiritual and moral decay? And, more important to us, how is living with integrity possible today? How can anyone—man or woman—live a life of consistent honesty and moral uprightness, when we, like Daniel, live in a thoroughly pagan society?

To answer these questions, we must look to Daniel's autobiography in the book of the Bible that bears his name. When we do, we can't help but detect—from the very first chapter—that prayer was a vital part of Daniel's secret to a life of holiness and integrity. We discover that Daniel was first and foremost a man of prayer.

Prayer in the Life of Daniel

I have often heard it said that sin will keep you from prayer, or prayer will keep you from sin. This seemed to be true regarding Daniel's life of integrity. Prayer played an important part in developing him into a man with a blameless life.

Daniel was habitual in prayer—Starting as a youth of 16 or 17, Daniel, along with three exiled friends, Shadrach, Meshach, and Abed-Nego, were devout in their religious practices, which involved habitual prayer. They saw God as their only protector and went to prayer to save their lives from the wrath of King Nebuchadnezzar.

Then, 65 years and two world empires later, Daniel found himself looking into the eyes of a den full of hungry lions. Daniel's life was in danger because of his habit of kneeling three times a day in front of an open window to pray (Daniel 6:10). He was condemned to death because he prayed!

Then in the sunset of his life, when he was about 82 years old, Daniel read a manuscript from the prophet Jeremiah that predicted that the Jews would be in captivity for 70 years. By Daniel's estimation, the 70 years were almost over. But as a world statesman, he saw no indications that suggested the return to Jerusalem was about to take place. So Daniel did what he had always done: He humbly came before God with a heartfelt plea, asking Him to work toward returning the Jews to their homeland (9:1-19).

A Lesson to Learn about Prayer

Integrity is hard to come by, but easily lost. And habitual prayer is an essential element in developing—and maintaining—a life of integrity. As a teen in a strange land, it would have been easy for Daniel to conform to the standards and customs of his new country, especially since he could lose his life if he defied the king's edicts. Besides, who would know or care?

But an unwavering commitment to God, nurtured by habitual prayer, had sustained and strengthened Daniel to successfully resist the world's temptations. And this habit and resistance lasted through the reigns of three different pagan empires.

Is prayer a habitual part of your life? Are you faithfully resisting the temptations of society? Or are you compromising in small or even big ways to the standards of your culture? Daniel's life illustrates the correlation between your prayer life and your public life. If you are presently praying on a regular basis, your resolve for God and His standards will be further strengthened. But if prayer is not a habit for you, don't wait to begin developing it. This world needs more Daniels—men and women of habitual prayer, men and women of remarkable integrity.

Daniel prayed in an emergency—Too many people wait for a crisis to hit before they start praying. Because Daniel's life was characterized by habitual prayer, he was prepared to act with confidence when a crisis came. How would you react if you opened the door to your house and you were greeted by a group of the king's executioners, who were there to kill you for no apparent reason? That's what happened to Daniel (2:14-15).

Armed with God's strength and wisdom, this teenager asked the king for time to understand and interpret a dream that had so disturbed the king that he ordered the deaths of all his wise men, which included Daniel. How could Daniel be so confident that God would reveal the secrets of King Nebuchadnezzar's dream to him? Only a person who has a close relationship with God through prayer could be prepared to make this kind of statement in the midst of such an extreme crisis.

A Lesson to Learn about Prayer

Emergency prayers are sometimes called "foxhole prayers." A foxhole prayer is a singular prayer by a soldier or anyone in the thick of battle or any life-threatening situation when he or she thinks they are about to die. In desperation, as a last resort, they pray. They make all sorts of vows to God, bargain with Him, and hope that their vows will move God to save their lives.

Daniel's prayer was definitely not a one-time foxhole prayer. His prayer was not the *result* of a crisis. No, it was a prayer in *response* to a crisis. It was the *result* of a habit of regular prayer.

Therefore, Daniel was calm in the midst of a do-or-die circumstance and gathered his three young friends to join him in prayer "that they might seek mercies from the God of heaven concerning this secret, so that Daniel and his companions might not perish with the rest of the wise men of Babylon" (Daniel 2:18).

Allow Daniel to be your prayer tutor. Start praying today, so that when the crisis or disaster comes tomorrow, you will face it with strength and courage. Any unwanted news becomes yet another occasion for you to exercise your privilege of again going confidently, through prayer, to God's throne of grace.

Daniel was a man of exacting prayer—He knew how to pray and what to pray for. In the midst of the crisis caused by the king's dream, Daniel did not pray in generalities. He prayed specifically, and he prayed precisely, and he prayed earnestly. He had two requests: That God would reveal the secret of the king's dream, and that God would preserve and protect Daniel and his three friends. God tells us that "in everything," whether it's a crisis or not, to "let your requests be made known to God" (Philippians 4:6).

Prayer is not merely giving God information about your needs. You don't need to "clue" Him in on what's happening. No, "your Father knows the things you have need of before you ask Him" (Matthew 6:8). Nor do you need to persuade God to hear you. His love for you does not need to be coaxed or induced. He is always available and with you. But His desire is that you still "ask, and it will be given to you; seek, and you will find; knock, and it will be open to you. For everyone who asks receives, and he who seeks finds, and to him who knocks it will be opened" (Matthew 7:7-8).

A Lesson to Learn about Prayer

God wants you to pray for specific needs. Why pray specifically? Because the Father delights in giving His children specific "good gifts" (verse 11). Then, too, there is the receiving of the good gifts. When you pray specifically and God responds, you receive confirmation that God truly does know your needs and will fulfill His promises to meet them.

Learn another lesson from Daniel: Because God knows your every need, there's no need to pray with "vain repetitions" (6:7). Like Daniel and his three friends, keep your prayers brief and specific. Then wait for God's specific reply.

Daniel prayed for his people—The prayer Daniel spoke in Daniel 9:1-19 was lifted to God because Daniel thought the time of the Jews' return to Jerusalem was near. He had read the predictions of the return of God's people, but he could not physically see how this could come about. Freedom did not seem to be drawing near. Daniel was concerned that maybe the people, and even he, were still in sin and, for whatever reason, God may have postponed the return of the Jews to their homeland. Confused, perplexed, and concerned, Daniel prayed. And in response, God not only gave Daniel an inspired vision of Israel and its future (verses 20-27), but He also gave Daniel a view of the future for all the nations down to the end times (12:1-3).

A Lesson to Learn about Prayer

As we continue to look at prayers of the men and women who knew God well, we repeatedly see intercession is an important and ongoing part of their lives and contributions to God's people. As each one of God's men and women faithfully came to God seeking His guidance, God placed His heart of love and concern for others into each of their hearts.

Daniel's prayer for the people of Israel was no exception. His own prayerfulness had given him a heart that was extremely burdened for his fellow Jews and their exiled state. What a great lesson Daniel teaches us about intercessory prayer! Praying for others should not be seen as an obligation but as opportunity to pray and see God's hand move on behalf of others in need. This should motivate us to be more consistent in intercession and ask God to give us a greater burden for the people around us.

Daniel prayed with the right attitude—Your attitude in prayer is extremely important. The *how* of prayer is more important than the *what*. Meaningful prayer is a matter of the heart, not the eloquence of the words. The words we pray are only the outward fruit of what God already sees within.

We've seen this right attitude throughout this book in the prayers of the men and women of the Bible. And now we see this right attitude again expressed as Daniel prays one of the greatest prayers recorded in all the Bible (Daniel 9). While his words were beautiful, in God's eyes, his attitude was what really counted:

- Daniel felt the need to pray to God—Burdened for his countrymen, Daniel purposed to set his "face toward the Lord God" (verse 3).

- Daniel made preparations to pray before God—He fasted before approaching God with his concerns. Then, clothed in sackcloth and with ashes sprinkled on his head, he prayed (verse 3).

- Daniel came before God with humility of heart—The three elements of fasting, sackcloth, and ashes indicated contriteness of heart.[32]

- Daniel came before God with a thankful heart—He expressed his thanks with these words: "O Lord, great and awesome God, who keeps His covenant and mercy with those who love Him, and with those who keep His commandments" (verse 4).

- Daniel came with a penitent heart—As Daniel began to pray, he made confession not only for the Jewish exiles, but also for himself: "We have sinned and committed iniquity, we have done wickedly and rebelled" (verse 5).

A Lesson to Learn about Prayer

If ever there was a Jew in Daniel's day who might not need to confess a multitude of sins, it was Daniel. God had declared him to be righteous (Ezekiel 14:14). And yet Daniel confessed his sinfulness and his need for God's forgiveness right along with his fellow Jews. Daniel prayed with openness and complete surrender to God and with an attitude of humility.

When you pray, what is your attitude? Do you examine your heart and confess your sin, or do you tend to blame others for your actions? Do you come into God's presence demanding this and that? Do you pray openly and honestly? The next time you pray, pause and prepare. Make sure you talk to God with the right attitude. Then be ready for God's reply. That was Daniel's experience: "While I was speaking, praying, and confessing my sin and the sin of my people...the man Gabriel... reached me" and said, "I have come to tell you" an answer (Daniel 9:20-23).

God's answers to your humble prayers probably won't involve major events such as those connected to Daniel and Israel, but they will be just as dramatic!

Daniel maintained the honor of the true God—Pagans in Daniel's day evaluated foreign gods by the prosperity of the people who worshiped that deity and by the successes of their armies. Because of this, Judah's God—the true God—did not measure up well in the sight of the Babylonians and the Medo-Persians. Their pagan deities appeared to be stronger.

God used Daniel, at least with the kings of the Babylonian and Medo-Persian empires, to partially alter the estimation of the God of Israel. Daniel was influential in two ways: Because of his integrity and wisdom, he was placed in high positions within the governments of these two great empires. In these respected positions, the kings and rulers observed the strength of character, power, wisdom, dignity, and personal concern of a man who worshiped the God of Israel.

Then, because of his righteous character, God used Daniel to interpret two of Nebuchadnezzar's dreams (2:24-45; 4:1-26) and read to Belshazzar the mysterious writing on the palace wall (5:13-30), and Daniel survived Darius's command that he be thrown into the lions' den (6:18-22). These supernatural interventions forced at least two of these pagan world rulers to give adoration to God. Hear their praise:

- Nebuchadnezzar—"Truly your God is the God of gods, the Lord of kings, and a revealer of secrets" (2:47).

- Nebuchadnezzar again—"I thought it good to declare the signs and wonders that the Most High God has worked for me. How great are His signs, and how mighty His wonders! His kingdom is an everlasting kingdom, and His dominion is from generation to generation" (4:2-3).

- Darius—"He is the living God, and steadfast forever; His kingdom is the one which shall not be destroyed, and His dominion shall endure to the end" (6:26).

A Lesson to Learn about Prayer

In most ways you and I are no different than Daniel. We live in a pagan society. The rich, famous, and powerful people around us see our God as powerless or even nonexistent. As with Daniel, God will do His part. But likewise, as with Daniel, you and I must do our part. We must strive to excel at whatever vocation, role, or life position God has placed us in. And most assuredly, we must strive to live a holy life, a life that honors God.

Take a page out of Daniel's life and become a man or woman of prayer. Then make sure that "whether you eat or drink, or whatever you do, do all to the glory of God" (1 Corinthians 10:31). These steps—prayer and your conduct—will definitely start you down a path of honoring God all the days of your life.

In spite of being taken away from home and family and being deported to a foreign land, Daniel held fast to his faith in God. With God's help and the transforming power of prayer, he conducted his life and business affairs with impeccable integrity. Daniel faithfully prayed and sought God's guidance and protection throughout his life. And God honored Daniel's prayers—He not only protected him and his three special friends and co-laborers, but also allowed Daniel to view His sovereign hand at work in the lives of kings, nations, and individuals.

No matter what your age or stage in life, Daniel provides a model for you. His faith and trust in God was consistent, even in the midst of—and in spite of—an inconsistent and pagan world. Following in Daniel's steps in the sinful world you live in will accelerate your own life of personal and godly integrity.

Prayer Principles for You—Integrity

Prayer results in inspired vision.

Without prayer, your spiritual sight is diminished. Your vision is blurred or even blinded to spiritual solutions. You quickly become discouraged and defeated. Problems appear as mountains too high to overcome. But through prayer, you begin to regain or sharpen your spiritual vision. You begin to see things through new eyes, through God's eyes. What previously appeared to be impossible will seem possible when you pray.

Daniel was a man of prayer, but at times he too needed his vision sharpened. As he prayed, God opened his spiritual eyes to the future. Are you facing an impossible situation today? Do the challenges facing you seem insurmountable? Through prayer, allow God to open your spiritual eyes to His great and awesome plans for you.

Prayer secures an instant audience with God.

You don't need to ask for an audience with God. All you have to do is open your heart and pray. Like Daniel, you will be immediately ushered into the throne room of the "God of heaven." You will be talking directly to the One who loves you, protects you, and desires to provide all your needs. You have the Lord Jesus Christ to thank for making this instant access to God possible.

Prayer results in inspired wisdom.

As you commune with God through prayer and study His Word, you will not only receive spiritual insight but also the wisdom to follow through on that insight. But if and when your understanding is lacking or unclear, all you need to do is ask for wisdom: "If any of you lacks wisdom, let him ask of God, who gives to all liberally and without reproach, and it will be given to him" (James 1:5).

No matter how well you know God, or how long you have walked with Him and served Him, or how much you have experienced with Him, you can still easily become overwhelmed. That's what happened to the godly and faithful Daniel at age 84 when he received yet another distressing prophetic vision from God. And he discovered, once again, that prayer results in inspired wisdom. You will always need God's wisdom to understand the things of God.

Prayer provides us with necessary strength.

When your strength for handling an issue or tragedy is sapped and your physical and emotional vitality has run out, pray. It is waiting on God through prayer that renews your strength. Through prayer, you "mount up with wings like eagles" (Isaiah 40:31). You exchange your weariness for God's strength. You experience the empowering hand of God. God's Spirit touches you and refreshes you. It is as if God is saying, "Peace be to you; be strong, yes, be strong!" (Daniel 10:19). Then you can get up from prayer and, with renewed vigor, face your problems. As Daniel stated to God, "You have strengthened me" (verse 19).

Prayer drives away fear.

How is it that Daniel faced trial after trial with full integrity and unwavering confidence? How is it that he never fell apart due to fear or dread? How is it that danger, executioners, and lions failed to touch him?

The answer, of course, is prayer. There is no better way to strengthen your faith and trust in God than to be faithful in prayer. Pray daily for courage and confidence, for prayer transforms fear into faith, and then faith fights your fear. Pray, as the disciples did, for God to increase your faith (Luke 17:5).

A Prayer for Integrity

Lord God, may the prayer of my heart always be the same—that I may be a person of integrity in all that I do. Before You and all others, may I be honest and morally upright. Today I acknowledge Your sovereign right to my life and willingly submit to Your leading.

Lord, Daniel was a man of integrity, and I desire to follow You in such a way that integrity will be evident in my life as well. Give me Your strength and Your guidance so that I can make godly choices and be a positive influence on those around me—starting at home with my family. Amen.[33]

10

Prayers to Grow in Worship

My soul magnifies the Lord,
And my spirit has rejoiced in God my Savior.
—LUKE 1:46-47

Can you recall the most meaningful worship experience you've been a part of? For me it occurred just a few years after the fall of communism in Russia. I was in Moscow to teach a two-week course for a group of missionary pastors. Over the weekend, I preached in a small church on the outskirts of the city.

The small hall where the congregation held its service was packed with people of all ages—elderly men and ladies as well as young men and women, all with hope in their eyes. Young and old alike were basking in their newfound freedom. They no longer had to worship in hidden corners for fear of persecution. They were free to openly and without reservation worship and fellowship together. And worship they did! For more than three hours these dear saints prayed, sang, gave testimony, participated in the Lord's table, and listened to me preach from God's Word. Even though I was witnessing this experience through an interpreter, still, I was deeply moved by their heartfelt worship.

The Nature of Worship

Worship is a privilege of the Christian faith. It is one way you and I can honor God and focus on Him. We can worship God in any place and at any time—even in a rented hall in Russia—because we worship God in spirit and in truth (John 4:23).

We can be thankful today that worshiping God is such a delight and a joy. By contrast, many of the great people of prayer that we've met in this book had quite different responses to their encounters with God:

- To Abraham, God appeared as "a smoking oven and a burning torch" as He gave a divine oath to fulfill His promises to Abraham (Genesis 15:17). Abraham's response? "A deep sleep fell upon Abram; and behold, horror and great darkness fell upon him" (verse 12).

- To Moses, God appeared in "a flame of fire from the midst of a bush" (Exodus 3:2). Moses' response? "Moses hid his face, for he was afraid to look upon God" (verse 6).

- To Job, God spoke from the midst of a whirlwind (Job 38:1). Job's response? "I abhor myself, and repent in dust and ashes" (42:6).

- To Daniel, God had "the appearance of lightning, his eyes like torches of fire, his arms and feet like burnished bronze in color, and the sound of his words like the voice of a multitude" (Daniel 10:6). Daniel's response? "I saw this great vision, and no strength remained in me; for my vigor was turned to frailty in me, and I retained no strength" (verse 8).

Worship was the natural response these great Bible figures had to their visions of God. They each approached God with respect and, in their own way, conveyed their unworthiness before a holy God. Their meetings with God and, in some cases, angelic beings, were frightening and literally drained them of all strength.

We too must approach God with honor and respect. He is Almighty God! But aren't you thankful that because of the death and resurrection of Jesus, your encounters with God don't have to be frightening experiences? Jesus' work on the cross has made it possible for you to come boldly into the presence of God through prayer. And we can praise and worship Him as often as we desire, and without fear.

Think about the relationship you have with God. Ponder on Him as "high and lifted up...holy, holy, holy...the LORD of hosts; the whole earth is full of His glory" (Isaiah 6:1,3). Then spend a few minutes worshiping God with prayer and praise.

Prayer in the Life of Mary

There's another whose life was characterized by prayer and worship. Her name was Mary. We first meet her as a teenage girl who lived 2000 years ago in a little insignificant town in Galilee, called Nazareth. Mary's worshipful attitude toward God provides us with yet another trait that should be a part of any man or woman who aspires to know God well through prayer.

Maybe, like me, you've wondered why there isn't more written in the Bible about the life of Mary. You would think that the mother of Jesus would have chapter after chapter in the Bible about her life. But surprisingly, there are just a few verses sprinkled through the gospels and the book of Acts that speak of Mary at all.

But are those verses ever meaningful! As you read them, especially those devoted to her remarks to the angel Gabriel (Luke 1:26-38) and her prayer of worship (verses 46-55), you begin to understand a little of the depth of maturity and godly understanding this teenager possessed. These verbal encounters provide great insight into the heart and soul of this remarkable woman.

In addition to these few spoken words, Mary's life itself reveals much about worship. For indeed, Mary's personal life as the mother of God's Son was one of daily worship for 30 years.

Mary exhibited a spirit of humility—Worship is the expression of respect and reverence toward a divine being, and humility is a key attitude for this expression. Mary first showed us her humility when she gave a positive and respectful response to Gabriel's declaration that she would conceive and "bring forth a Son" (verse 31). She said, "Behold the maidservant of the Lord!"

(verse 38). Mary saw herself as nothing more than a female slave who was ready to do the bidding of her master.

After her encounter with the angel Gabriel and a journey south to a city in Judah, Mary arrived at her cousin Elizabeth's home (1:39). Upon seeing Mary, Elizabeth gave her a God-inspired blessing, which prompted Mary's "Magnificat," in which she exhibited humility as she lifted up a prayer of praise (verses 46-55):

- Humility responds appropriately—"My spirit has rejoiced" (verse 47). Mary had expected nothing, so she could appreciate the blessing God was bestowing on her.

- Humility realizes its need—Mary rejoiced in "God my Savior" (verse 47). Even though all generations would call her blessed, Mary had no illusions as to her spiritual condition. She knew she was a sinner who needed a Savior.

- Humility remembers its position—"He has regarded the lowly state of His maidservant" (verse 48). Mary remembered her position, both socially and spiritually. She was socially on the bottom tier, and spiritually ready and willing to serve God as a servant. This was exactly where God wanted her. In this position, He could honor her, for humility remembers its position and is ready to be used as needed. What God was doing in Mary's life would have a profound effect on the world and all future generations.

- Humility recognizes its provider—"He who is mighty...holy is His name" (verse 49). A humble person like Mary has

only one direction to look: up. Mary recognized who it was
that was at work in her life.

- Humility rejoices in its provision—"He who is mighty has
done great things for me" (verse 49). Mary not only recognized that God was working in her life, but also rejoiced in
what God was about to do.

Think back over the people of prayer we've met along the way
in this book—people like you and me who experienced God's
transforming power in daily life. Wouldn't you agree that humility
was a trait common to all of them? For example:

- *Abraham*—"bowed himself to the ground" and described
himself as "but dust and ashes" in the presence of the Lord
(Genesis 18:2,27).

- *Moses*—"was very humble, more than all the men who were
on the face of the earth" (Numbers 12:3). Because of this,
God said, "I speak with him face to face...and he sees the
form of the LORD" (12:8).

- *Hannah*—referred to herself as a "maidservant" (1 Samuel
1:11). Hannah, like Mary, saw herself as a servant ready to
fulfill the wishes of her Lord.

- *Job*—repented of complaining, questioning, and challenging
God's wisdom and justice, and in humility said, "I abhor
myself, and repent in dust and ashes" (Job 42:6).

- *David*—in his prayer of repentance understood that
God didn't want external ritual without genuine, humble

repentance. "You do not desire sacrifice, or else I would give it; You do not delight in burnt offering. The sacrifices of God are a broken spirit, a broken and a contrite heart" (Psalm 51:16-17).

Humility and prayer are co-contributors in the lives of God's people. A heart that is humble is a heart that prays. And conversely, a heart that prays is a heart that is humble.

A Lesson to Learn about Prayer

Do you yearn to be a man or woman of prayer? Then cultivate humility. How do you do this? Have a servant's heart. Keep a short record of sin with God. Confess often. Walk by the Spirit (Galatians 5:16). And, of course, pray! Prayer is an act of humility in itself. Prayer is the recognition of your utter dependence on God. The proud cannot pray. The arrogant will not pray. Only the humble want to—and do—pray. Acknowledge your humility right now by falling on your knees and praying.

Mary gave the right response to revelation—For centuries, every young Jewish girl dreamed of being the most blessed of women. Who would this fortunate woman be? A ruler's daughter? The Messiah must come from an aristocratic family, right? Or maybe the Messiah would be born into the home of a rich merchant. The Messiah should possess wealth and power, right? Wrong!

God chose Mary to be that favored one. She was a simple

peasant girl. She had no money, no position in society. In fact, she had no husband! So why Mary? What was her one and only qualification? She had "found favor with God" (Luke 1:30). She had not earned this favor, nor did she possess any special righteous virtue. And she too, according to her own words, was in need of a Savior (verse 47). God, in His sovereign wisdom, had simply chosen her out of all the young Jewish women of Judah to be the mother of His Son.

How would she respond to the revelation that God had chosen her to be the mother of the Messiah? She was just a teenager—the offer was overwhelming! After all, she might not want to pay the high price of obedience. But we know the answer, don't we? Yet it's a reasonable question to ask because many other great Bible personalities who were older and should have been more mature responded to God's revelations quite differently than Mary. For instance:

- Sarah— "laughed" when she heard the revelation that she would have a son in her old age (Genesis 18:9-15).

- Moses—gave every excuse he could think of before finally relenting and reluctantly accepting God's plan for his life (Exodus 3:11–4:17).

- Zacharias—who earlier had also received a visit from Gabriel, asked for proof of the revelation that his wife, Elizabeth, would conceive in her old age: "How shall I know this?" (Luke 1:18).

- Mary—on the other hand, responded with complete trust. She accepted what God was going to do. Her only question was about the process: "How can this be, since I do not know a man?" (verse 34). Her final response revealed her faith in God.

Many people today are waiting on a "Gabriel" to bring them a revelation from God for their life. Like Zacharias, they are waiting for visible proof. But did the presence of an angel (visible proof) make any difference in Zacharias's response to the revelation he was given? No. In disbelief, Zacharias wanted even more proof! Unbelief can never receive enough proof.

But faith, on the other hand, requires no proof. Mary understood that God was going to perform a miracle. She didn't need proof. Her faith accepted the angel's statement. She merely asked how this miraculous event could occur because she was a virgin.

A Lesson to Learn about Prayer

Today God speaks to us not through angels, but as we read our Bibles. The Bible is God-breathed (2 Timothy 3:16)—it is the inspired Word of the living God. Therefore its very words are "living and powerful and sharper than any two-edged sword, piercing even to the division of soul and spirit, and of joints and marrow, and is a discerner of the thoughts and intents of the heart" (Hebrews 4:12).

Does Mary's response give you any insight as to how you should respond to God as you read His Word? Given the examples of how others responded to God, we now know not to laugh like Sarah did. Not to make excuses like Moses did. Not to rationalize like Jeremiah did. Not to ask for proof or reassurance like Zacharias did.

Even when what God promises seems to be humanly impossible, remember that "with God all things are possible" (Matthew 19:26). Don't respond in unbelief. Like Mary, respond in faith: "Let it be to me according to your word" (Luke 1:38).

Mary worshiped with others—What's special about worship is that it can be performed alone, or...

—*with another*, as happened with Mary and her cousin, Elizabeth. Elizabeth, filled with the Holy Spirit, started the worship experience immediately upon Mary's arrival with her own exultation of praise. She "spoke out with a loud voice" (verse 42). God's Spirit had given her an extraordinary grasp of the significance of Mary's pregnancy. Elizabeth prophesied, "Blessed are you among women, and blessed is the fruit of your womb!" (verse 42). And she too, like Mary, exhibited worship's key attitude— humility—as she exclaimed, "Why is this granted to me, that the mother of my Lord should come to me?" (verse 43).

—*with others*, as in corporate worship with a body of believers. The last glimpse of Mary in the Bible shows her together with a group of fellow believers in the upper room (Acts 1:12-14). This band of 120 believers in the risen Christ had come together and "all continued with one accord in prayer and supplication." They were obediently waiting for the coming of the Spirit and the birth of the church (verse 5).

A Lesson to Learn about Prayer

Worship is the appropriate response to a holy God. Prayer and praise are the vehicles you can use to express your love and adoration for Him. Mary's life of continual worship, from start to finish, provides a sterling example of how you should live. Do you know someone or some others with whom you can enjoy times of worship and fellowship? Join with them in mutual worship, and thank God for these precious shared times.

Mary's heart was saturated with God's Word—Some have wondered how the young Mary was able to speak the incredibly insightful words that made up her prayer—her Magnificat—of pure worship (Luke 1:46-55). Obviously God's Spirit was involved. But she also must have been taught from an early age to love God and His Word. Her brief years of study had made the Scriptures alive to her and etched them on her heart and soul.

From her storehouse of truth, Mary delivered her famous and profound Magnificat. Its entirety exalted the covenant-keeping God of Israel—"He has helped His servant Israel" (verse 54). Her prayer was filled with allusions to and quotations of the law, the psalms, and the prophets. The Old Testament themes of redemption, freedom, and justice flowed through her worship. Mary focused on God's power, holiness, and mercy. Her confidence in God came from her knowledge of His character, and her worship revealed a heart and mind that were saturated with God.

A Lesson to Learn about Prayer

One of the great benefits of the Scriptures is that they strengthen and give structure to your prayers. God's Word provides a tool you can use in prayer. Through prayerful attention to Mary's Magnificat, you can learn how better to communicate with God. And like Mary, you can learn to make the words of Scripture a part of your own worship prayers.

Are you saturating your heart and mind with God's Word? Are you hiding it in your heart? Fill your mind with God's mind and, like Mary, you won't be able to help but "magnify the Lord" in prayer and praise.

Mary had faith in God—From her first encounter with God's messenger, Mary exhibited a strong confidence in God and His dealings with her. You would never know she was but a teenager by the way she responded with complete trust and obedience. Elizabeth praised Mary's faith in God in this way: "Blessed is she who believed, for there will be a fulfillment of those things which were told her from the Lord" (verse 45).

Faith is only as valid as the object of faith. The object of Mary's faith is expressed in her Magnificat. It was her mighty and merciful God, the Holy One, the Helper in times of need, the God of the covenant, the One she called "God my Savior." One Bible commentator points out the "profession of faith" which runs through these lines from beginning to end, creates "a good reason for calling her poem 'Mary's Song of Faith.'"[34]

A Lesson to Learn about Prayer

Wars and rumors of war and crime and violence are everywhere. We live in fearful times, and it's easy to get caught up in fear and paranoia. You and I can become as fearful as those around us who have "no hope and [are] without God" (Ephesians 2:12). But it doesn't have to be that way. Take a lesson from a teenage girl. Develop a better understanding of the trustworthy character and nature of God. Rehearse with God His glory and might. Thank Him for His holiness and His mercy. Then, after a time in prayer, rise up in faith and live with confidence and to the glory of God! God is powerful. "He who is mighty has done great things" (Luke 1:49). What fears can you face today with God's help?

The Bible portrays Mary as a woman "blessed among women" —not as one to be worshiped, but a faithful, humble worshiper. Her unique blessing came as she was chosen by God to bear His Son. But Mary had a hard life. Although she was blessed by God, Simeon predicted to her that "a sword will pierce through your own soul" (Luke 2:35). And those piercing words came true on the day when, in agony and grief, Mary stood at the foot of the cross and witnessed the death of her firstborn as a despised criminal (John 19:25). Yet Mary bore the pain in her life with quiet humility and submission, never failing to worship and praise the God she believed in and trusted. Mary's remarkable but humble life gives you and me a magnificent model of prayer and worship.

Prayer Principles for You—Worship

Prayer prepares the way to accept God's will.

A person's life is not made up of segments, compart-
ments, or stages. Life is one continuous, uncut ribbon.
And that uncut ribbon, for a believer, is a constant opportunity to choose to follow God's will. God's will may come
in a dramatic moment when a critical decision must be
made. Or it may arrive in the little and supposedly routine choices that each day presents. But in either case,
whether the dramatic or the routine, prayer provides the
line of communication that will help enable you to determine God's will.

Praying regularly helps to transform your heart and
mind. It puts you in the habit of accepting God's will
each day and each step of the way. Then when something
earth-shattering occurs, as happened to Mary when the
angel announced God's will for her, you can more easily
accept God's plan. And even though that plan may
require changes on your part, prayer enables you to
humbly receive God's latest step in your ribbon of life.

Prayer cultivates a heart of obedience.

The goal of your prayers is to glorify God as you obediently seek to line up your will with His. When you go
to God in prayer, be prepared to echo Mary's submissive
spirit to whatever God reveals as His will: "Behold the
[servant] of the Lord! Let it be to me according to your

word" (Luke 1:38). Obedience is never easy, but each and every time you come before God with the attitude of a submissive servant, you are cultivating a heart of obedience.

Prayer is an opportunity to praise and worship.

Prayer opens up opportunity after opportunity to worship God as your creator and to praise Him for His goodness and mercy. You can always find something good in your life to praise God for (Romans 8:28). Thanksgiving and adoration are vital parts of the prayer process. They give you a chance to respond positively to God's work in your life. They allow you, like Mary, to magnify the Lord. Let your praise and worship flow!

Prayer is a reflective exercise.

Prayer is a serious discipline that requires thoughtful preparation. You would never think of going to your boss with an idea until you were ready to make a clear, logical presentation. Nor would you meet with an important public official to discuss a social concern without a plan or strategy. So it is with coming to God in prayer. Mary-the-worshiper is pictured as meditative, as reflective. She "pondered" all that took place and made sure she "kept all these things...in her heart" (Luke 2:19). Meaningful prayer requires that you reflect on who it is you are addressing—God—and what you are requesting, and why.

It is a reflective attitude of worship—a desire to fully appreciate God's work in your life—that separates your life from the ordinary and transforms it into the extraordinary. "Be still, and know that I am God" (Psalm 46:10) is a command that should stop you in your tracks. So be still. Spend time alone in prayerful worship and praise to God. Ponder His will for your life and His work in you.

Prayer generates spiritual strength.

One of the great mysteries of prayer is that it truly strengthens, refreshes, and rejuvenates one's soul. Prayer is a spiritual discipline that generates multiple spiritual results. Communing with God fortifies you. Talking things over with Him reminds you that He is with you, even in the midst of pain and sorrow. Knowing that you can go to God through prayer at any time and anywhere and when no one else can help gives you strength in your hour of need. As you pray and wait on the Lord, you will find yourself rejuvenated. You will discover you can run and not become weary, and walk and not faint (Isaiah 40:31).

A Prayer for Worship

Dear God my Savior, I am moved—and humbled—by Mary's outburst of praise as she magnified You and rejoiced in the work that You were accomplishing on Your people's behalf. May I seek to fill my days with worship, to remember that I should not focus on what *I* am, but on who *You* are. Looking to You and taking notice of Your magnificent works and promises gives me strength and resolve to face this day and every day with peace and assurance—and hope. Amen.[35]

11

Prayers to Grow in Passion

*For this reason I bow my knees to the Father of our Lord
Jesus Christ, from whom the whole family in heaven and
earth is named, that He would grant you, according to
the riches of His glory, to be strengthened with might
through His Spirit in the inner man.*

—EPHESIANS 3:14-16

I t was a brilliant noonday sun that beat down on a band of
men as they neared Damascus. They had endured a long,
hard journey, but Saul and his henchman were ready to
fulfill their assignment. They had been commissioned by the high
priest in Jerusalem to go to Damascus and arrest those "who were
of the Way" (Acts 9:2)—the Jesus-followers—and bring them back
for trial.

But suddenly a light brighter than the sun appeared, blinding Saul. In his darkened state he heard a voice from heaven saying, "Saul, Saul, why are you persecuting Me?" Saul, the Hebrew name of the soon-to-become-apostle Paul, covered his head with his hands as he asked in bewilderment, "Who are You, Lord?" (verses 4-5).

To Paul's amazement, the voice speaking identified Himself as the One whom those belonging to "the Way" worshiped and claimed had risen from the grave—"I am Jesus, whom you are persecuting" (verse 5).

But...this Jesus was supposed to be dead! He had been crucified by the Romans years before. Yet now Paul was hearing Jesus speak. In fear and astonishment, he asked, "Lord, what do You want me to do?" Paul was given his first instructions by Jesus Himself: "Arise and go into the city, and you will be told what you must do" (verse 6).

At that moment the zealous persecutor of God's people became a passionate preacher of the gospel—the good news of the risen Savior, Jesus Christ. Paul's zeal went from one direction to another. He had formerly been committed to God's Law as it was understood by the rabbis and Jewish leaders of his day (Philippians 3:4-6). And he was fervently opposed to this new religious sect called "the Way." But now Paul's zeal was *for* Christ, and not *against* Him. Paul had a new purpose, a new vision, a new passion. In short, he was to go and preach the gospel to the Gentiles (Acts 9:15).

Living with Passion and Purpose

Without a passion for something, you drift aimlessly through life. You are like a ship without a rudder, a sailor without a compass. But once you fix your sights on a direction, you can focus all your energies on that goal. This energy is what passion is all about. This intense drive for something or someone is what gets you out of bed in the morning, It's what keeps you going through your day. And it's what keeps you up late at night. It creates energy and gives your life meaning.

That's exactly what happened to Paul. Passion for the Savior gave him the drive to accomplish extraordinary feats for Jesus during the next 25 years. Paul stated his passion for Jesus in this way: "that I may know Him and the power of His resurrection, and the fellowship of His sufferings, being conformed to His death" (Philippians 3:10). Can you feel his intensity? With this all-out commitment to serve his Lord, Paul pressed forward in his quest to be obedient to God's call on his life (Philippians 3:14). Paul's passion for Jesus was what motivated him to...

- preach night and day to the people and their leaders in Ephesus (Acts 20:31)

- expend his life until he could declare at its end, "I have fought the good fight, I have finished the race, I have kept the faith" (2 Timothy 4:7)

- be a faithful steward of God's purpose for his life (1 Corinthians 4:2)

Prayer is essential for determining God's purpose and igniting the passion for accomplishing God's purpose.

Prayer in the Life of Paul

The focus of Paul's life and ministry was prayer. One scholar estimated the value of prayer in Paul's life in this way: "Paul's course was more distinctly shaped and his career rendered more powerfully successful by prayer than by any other force."[36] What can we learn from this prayer giant?

Paul prayed for direction—Paul was an extremely driven man. He had been commissioned by Jesus Himself to take the gospel to the Gentiles. Unlike those who think they don't need wisdom or input, Paul sought help. He not only functioned as a team player along with Barnabas at the church in Antioch, but he also was open to God's direction through his fellow leaders as they all prayed. The Bible says "as they ministered to the Lord and fasted, the Holy Spirit said, 'Now separate to Me Barnabas and Saul for the work to which I have called them'" (Acts 13:1-2). The leaders' prayers did not set Paul apart, but rather, they served to affirm the Spirit's choice. Therefore, Paul and Barnabas could go on their mission with full confidence that God was guiding them.

A Lesson to Learn about Prayer

Praying for direction should be an important practice in your life. Nothing is too insignificant to pray over. If you believe God is leading you in a certain direction, wait for confirmation. Ask the leadership of your church to pray along with you. Then you can proceed with confidence as God guides you through answered prayer.

Paul prayed and fasted—Fasting was part of the prayer life
of many of the remarkable people in the Bible. Recall Hannah,
Samuel, Nehemiah, Daniel, and, as we'll see in the next chapter,
Jesus.[37] The preparation and eating of food requires a significant
portion of a person's day. Therefore fasting gives people extra
time to pray, to consider and confess areas of sin, and to enter
into a more sensitive posture of body, mind, and spirit toward
receiving God's direction. Hunger, too, reinforces a sense of
repentance and reminds us of our dependence upon God.

Like the men and women who had gone before them, Paul and
Barnabas combined prayer and fasting when facing important
decisions. The ministry team at Antioch prayed and fasted as a
routine part of the spiritual discipline of leading the church. And
when the Holy Spirit spoke concerning the separation of Paul and
Barnabas for special ministry, the leadership again went to prayer
with fasting and sought God's direction before sending these two
on their important missionary venture (Acts 13:2-3).

Another time of prayer and fasting came at the end of Paul
and Barnabas's first missionary tour. They had spent two years
establishing churches in the area, and now had to leave. Ongoing
leadership in their absence was critical. And, as these two men
had done before, they prayed and fasted to affirm and commend
to the Lord the elders they had appointed to positions of leadership (Acts 14:23).

A Lesson to Learn about Prayer

The spiritual discipline of fasting is helpful today as we
too seek God's will and direction. Adding fasting to your

prayer life introduces an element of further seriousness to your prayers. Too often it's easy to come casually to God in prayer. On some occasions we may even have a degree of superficiality in our prayers. But when you determine to fast in conjunction with your praying, you are expressing a desire to be more focused upon God.

So, on those occasions when your heart is especially burdened, or when significant decisions need to be made, why not intensify the seriousness of your prayers by fasting?

Paul's prayers were strategic—Paul had a love for all believers, both those he knew personally and those he knew only by report (Colossians 1:3-4). He was concerned about their physical state, and more importantly, their spiritual well-being. Here are a few of the spiritual concerns Paul prayed for in Colossians 1:9-12. They are the same ones Paul would have for you and me today:

- to possess a knowledge of God's will
- to obtain wisdom and spiritual understanding
- to walk worthy of the Lord
- to be fruitful in every good work
- to be strengthened by God's glorious power
- to be patient and longsuffering
- to have a thankful heart

Have you perfected these elements of spiritual maturity? Then here are a few additional areas of spiritual development Paul prayed for among Christians:

- He prayed for our purity in body, soul, and spirit (1 Thessalonians 5:23-24).

- He prayed that we would be filled with the fruits of righteousness...which are to the glory and praise of God (Philippians 1:11).

- He prayed that we would be strengthened with power in the inner man (Ephesians 3:16).

- He prayed that we would experience the fullness of God (Ephesians 3:18-19).

- He prayed that we would be like-minded and glorify God with one mind and one mouth (Romans 15:5-6).

A Lesson to Learn about Prayer

What is the focus of your prayers? Is it on the temporal and physical matters? Are your prayers for yourself and others filled with issues of health, home, and finances? These are important issues to be sure, but they are not the highest priorities on God's scale of importance. When weighed on an eternal scale, they fall far short. (And, by the way, didn't God already promise to take care of what you eat, drink, and wear—of your physical needs—in Matthew 6:31? And didn't Paul say God would supply all your needs in Philippians 4:19?)

When you pray, take a lesson from Paul, and pray strategically. Pray for spiritual needs. Let your prayers be filled with concerns for salvation, spiritual growth, wisdom, discernment, and conduct. Allow your prayers to take on eternal qualities. The physical world is passing away, and the spiritual realm is where the real battles are fought— battles for the heart and soul. So pray accordingly.

Paul's prayers were continuous—Paul was a man who practiced what he preached. He exhorted the Thessalonian believers to "pray without ceasing" (1 Thessalonians 5:17). Paul had already told these people that he prayed "night and day" to return to them and give them further teaching (3:10). So, when he told them to "pray without ceasing," Paul was asking them to follow his example.

What does it mean to "pray without ceasing," or to "always keep on praying" (TLB)? The phrase "without ceasing means 'constant' and defines prayer not as some perpetual activity of kneeling and interceding but as a way of life marked by a continual attitude of prayer."[38] Paul exhibited this continual attitude of prayer himself as he prayed...

- by the riverside with a group of women (Acts 16:13)

- in a dungeon with his feet in stocks (Acts 16:25)

- with the Ephesian elders on the beach (Acts 20:36)

- with a group of disciples in Troas, again on the beach (Acts 21:5)

- while in a storm at sea (Acts 27:23-25)

- while in prison for several years[39]

A Lesson to Learn about Prayer

Prayer is a spiritual discipline that is difficult for even the most devout Christians to practice on a truly consistent basis. It demands time and requires focus, which is hard for modern minds and lifestyles to incorporate. To pray also requires us to overcome our natural tendency to try and come up with our own solutions. Prayer tries our patience. We dislike waiting on God's answers. So we try to manipulate our situation by coming up with our own quick answers.

Don't let the struggle to pray discourage you. Ask God to keep you from being distracted by the world around you, to give you a God-focus. To give you receptivity to His will. To help you look at life through the lens of Scripture. And to help you wait patiently for His answers. Then, like Paul, you will develop a "praying always" attitude.

Paul's prayers were for other people—Like the other people of prayer in the Bible, Paul was an intercessor. His writings are filled with intercessory prayers on behalf of others. Almost every one of Paul's New Testament letters begins with "I make mention of you in my prayers."[40] He must have had a remarkable prayer list!

Paul's prayers were not only for fellow believers, but also for those in governmental authority. Paul never forgot that he was a citizen of the world, and that citizenship, like every other privilege, imposed responsibilities. So Paul prayed for those in authority—that they would rule well so believers could better "lead a quiet and peaceable life in all godliness and reverence" (1 Timothy 2:2).

A Lesson to Learn about Prayer

As we have already seen, Paul prayed unceasingly for others, most of whom he had never met or seen. It's hard enough to pray consistently for people you know. Just imagine doing that for people you don't know! But that's Paul's lesson to us. He saw intercession as a powerful aspect of his ministry. It didn't matter where he was—in a prison or by a river—Paul could still pray for others. And it didn't matter if he knew them or not. What mattered was that they needed his prayers, whether they were believers in the church or unbelievers in authority.

And it's the same today. It doesn't matter who a person is or where you are. You should be continually praying for others. What matters is that people everywhere need your prayers. Why not start your own prayer list today?

Paul asked for prayer from others—Paul spent his life praying for others. He was an encourager to many. But he also understood that the power of prayer could and should work on his behalf too. Paul's requests for prayer were never selfish, but always for the progress of the gospel.

Even though Paul was the mighty apostle, preacher, and missionary who had worked countless miracles, had the Lord speak to him through visions, and had been a vehicle for God's Word to the church, Paul pleaded for others to pray for him. He asked for prayer from:

- The church in Rome—"Strive together with me in prayers to God *for me*, that I may be delivered from those in Judea who do not believe, and that my service for Jerusalem may be acceptable" (Romans 15:30-31).

- The church in Corinth—"You also helping together in prayer *for us*, that thanks may be given by many persons on our behalf for the gift granted to us through many" (2 Corinthians 1:11).

- The church in Ephesus—"Praying always with all prayer and supplication in the Spirit, being watchful...with all perseverance and supplication for all the saints—and *for me*, that utterance may be given to me, that I may open my mouth boldly to make known the mystery of the gospel" (Ephesians 6:18).

- The church in Colosse—"Praying also *for us,* that God would open *to us* a door for the word, to speak the mystery of Christ" (Colossians 4:3).

A Lesson to Learn about Prayer

Paul wrote about fighting against "principalities, against powers, against the rulers of the darkness of this age, against spiritual hosts of wickedness in the heavenly places" (Ephesians 6:12). He understood that there is a fierce spiritual battle being fought in our world and that each believer needs the prayer support of others. He understood that there is spiritual strength and solidarity in the uniting of our prayers.

Paul's lesson to us is clear. Just as Paul was dependent on the prayers of God's people to give his ministry success, we too should request and depend on the prayers of others for our life and ministry. Don't try to wage the spiritual battle alone. Seek out others to pray for and with you as you "fight the good fight of faith" (1 Timothy 6:12).

Paul's prayers were in faith—As you read through Paul's prayers, you can't help but notice that they were always uttered with complete confidence. Paul believed in answered prayer. So it's no surprise that in the midst of a violent storm at sea while on the way to Rome, Paul stood up and proclaimed with bold confidence and great faith that everyone would be saved.

How could he make such a statement? Because God's angel confirmed to Paul that he would indeed make it safely to Rome to stand before Caesar. It's highly probably that Paul had been praying throughout the 14 days of the storm and that the angelic messenger's appearance was God's answer to his prayers. Paul and the entire ship's company had almost given up hope that they would live through the violent storm. Yet in faith Paul declared, "I believe God that it will be just as it was told me" (Acts 27:25).

A Lesson to Learn about Prayer

Faith is an essential element in prayer. Faith is the reason you pray in the first place. Faith believes that God hears and will answer your prayers according to His will and your best interests. Faith looks at the hopeless and, without any doubt, asks of God (James 1:6). Faith looks at the impossible and prayerfully asks for the possible, believing that God is able.

Paul believed that in God's divine economy his prayers, somehow and in some way, made a difference. Do you share Paul's great faith in God and prayer? If not, quickly ask Him to help you in your unbelief.

Paul is among one of the more significant figures the Christian faith has ever produced. He wrote 13 of the 27 books of the New Testament. His writings contribute many of the essential doctrinal truths of the Christian faith. He was a pioneer missionary and church planter. And the amazing part of his incredible ministry is that Paul accomplished all this in about 25 years.

What were the key factors in Paul's productive life? First, Paul had a passion for serving his Savior. From the moment Jesus spoke to him on the Damascus Road, Paul was totally committed to fulfilling Jesus' call on his life. Nothing was allowed to keep him from discharging his labor of love, his service for his Lord.

Second, Paul's passion for serving Christ was supplemented by his passion for prayer. Prayer was as important to Paul as breathing is to you and me. He prayed constantly. He prayed for those he knew personally and for those he knew only by reputation. Any and all became names for his prayer list.

If you are running short on spiritual passion, let Paul be your model, your mentor. Ask the Father to give you Paul's great passion for His Son. Ask God to give you Paul's heart for people and a greater passion for prayer.

Prayer Principles for You—Passion

Prayer is to be with understanding.

Prayer is a conversation with God. But often we can't think of anything to say to God, so we ramble. Or we have so much on our hearts that we go off in 30 different directions in the same prayer. Paul's prayers are a study in thoughtful, serious, heartfelt petition. He understood something of the nature and power of God, and prayed like a lawyer carefully pressing his case before a judge— fervently, yet with direction. Don't fail to pray, but do study God's Word and the prayers of God's men and women to learn how to pray with better understanding.

Prayer is assisted by the Holy Spirit.

The Holy Spirit is a vital member of your prayer team. All believers are called to be "praying in the Holy Spirit" (Jude 20), to pray consistently in the power of the Spirit. This is made possible by God's Spirit living in you. Your need of the Holy Spirit's aid in prayer is great. Even when you are not sure how to pray, the ministry of the Spirit is there to help (Romans 8:26). Often believers are inclined to ask for things that would be harmful. So, knowing fully the mind and will of the Father, the Spirit assists you in your prayers by interceding for you and purifying the motives behind your prayer requests.

Prayer is to focus on spiritual concerns.

Prayer is heavenly business. When you pray, you are asking God for His will to be done on earth as it has already been decreed in heaven. Even though the earthly realm where you live is important to you, it's not the chief concern of the Father. Paul showed us this truth as he focused his prayers on the spiritual realm. Only once did Paul mention a personal need for physical health. Otherwise, earthly and temporal matters are scarcely mentioned. Physical concerns have their place in intercession, but they should always take a secondary position to praying for the spiritual concerns of others.

Prayer is not always answered immediately.

God's answers to your prayers may take years to come. But your role is to pray and trust that God will give the answer at the earliest moment consistent with His purposes. A prayer, once prayed, passes out of the finite realm and into the infinite, into the realm of God, and it's possible you may never know how your prayer was answered on this side of heaven.

It's hard to persevere in prayer when no response seems to come. But be assured no prayer is ever offered in vain. If you believe your prayer is within the scope of God's love and according to His will, then pray on. The answer may be postponed, but it will be forthcoming. The blessed answer has been consigned, and the delivery date has been noted in God's divine log book. It will come at just the right moment, when it is needed the most.

A Prayer for Passion

Heavenly Father, like the apostle Paul I come before You as "a bondservant of Jesus Christ." How I thank You for Paul's fiery passion for You, which was so often revealed through his prayers. Because of Paul's all-consuming love for You, I can better articulate praise to You, my heavenly Father, and to Your Son, the Lord Jesus Christ. You have blessed me with "every spiritual blessing in the heavenly places" because I am Your child through Jesus, my Savior. I praise You that these blessings include Christ's righteousness, His access to Your throne of mercy, His intercession on my behalf, and ultimately His glory. In every circumstance—including my suffering—grant me the grace to praise You, for "You are worthy, O Lord, to receive glory and honor and power." Amen.[41]

12

Following Jesus' Example
in Prayer

Jesus lifted up His eyes and said,
"Father, I thank You that You have heard Me.
And I know that You always hear Me."
— JOHN 11:41-42

As we conclude our study of knowing God through prayer, I can't help but recall my trips to India. It seems each of these trips provided a new opportunity for knowing God as He answered our prayers on many occasions.

Take, for instance, my first trip to India. Those in my mission team arrived in Singapore as a stopover. We were to fly out the next afternoon...or so we thought. On that next afternoon we

197

arrived at the airport only to be told the plane had already left. How could we have made such a gross error? So there we stood, dumbfounded, in the middle of a vast international airport. There was no way we could contact our host in India (who had to travel two hours by bus, taxi, and auto-rickshaw to meet us at the airport in Bombay. And it would be another ten years before he had a telephone line installed into his home!).

What were we to do? We were all aware that another plane would fly to Bombay the next day, but would Chris, our host, be there? Would he figure out what might have happened to us and wait, or would we get off the plane in a strange land with very different customs and have no one to meet us? As we huddled in the middle of that bustling Asian airport, we went to prayer. "O Lord, somehow in Your great providence You have allowed us to miss this plane. What do we do now?" As we finished our prayers asking God for direction, a strange peace came over me. I knew exactly what we should do. I confidently blurted out, "We should take the next flight to Bombay. Chris will be there when we arrive."

And sure enough, Chris was there, smiling as we came out into the blazing summer sun. This was a marvelous confirmation of our prayers, and made us greatly aware that God had gone before us and had opened the way for us to minister in His strength and power. And that's exactly what happened. We had two incredibly productive weeks of Spirit-led ministry.

As I look back at that missed plane and that special prayer meeting in the middle of Changi Airport, I can't help but believe that the assurance we all sensed at that time had resulted from praying for God's direction through an "oversight" on our part.

To a degree, that assuredness of answered prayer that we sensed was the same assurance Jesus knew all through His life of ministry. Jesus summed up His open line of communication with His Father when He said, "I know that You always hear Me" (John 11:42).

The Perfect Model in Prayer

"I Want to Be Like Jesus" is the title of a hymn that should properly reflect our goal when it comes to prayer. What a marvelous goal it is for us to desire that, like Jesus, our hearts would be pure and free of sin and, therefore, our prayers would always be heard (Psalm 66:18). And like Jesus, we would find our prayers answered because we would be praying in the will of the Father (1 John 5:14).

Jesus lived in the spirit of prayer. He could be alone with the Father in a crowd or in a secluded place. Prayer was His life, His habit. He prayed in every situation, in every emergency, and at every opportunity for all issues. And He prayed for the sheer joy of talking with His Father. Looking at the life and prayers of Jesus provides us with a perfect end to this book. Let's see now what we can learn from Him.

Jesus prayed before important events or decisions—How do you deal with key events in your life? And how do you make your decisions? Do you fret and worry? Do you stew and pace? Whether it's an important event you are facing or a decision you need to make, follow Jesus' model. The Gospels—Matthew, Mark, Luke, John—show us Jesus at prayer before major events and significant decisions such as these:

—The beginning of His ministry. Jesus' baptism was a significant event in His life and ministry. This public ceremony marked the formal beginning of Jesus' public service (Acts 1:21-22). How did Jesus approach this time in His life? We find Him offering up His first recorded instance of prayer: "It came to pass that Jesus also was baptized; and while He prayed, the heaven was opened. And the Holy Spirit descended" (Luke 3:21-22).

—The choosing of His leaders. Jesus had many disciples, but He desired to choose 12 as leaders, as apostles—"sent ones"—and give them special authority to deliver His message to the world. This event marked the beginning of the focused training of 12 men to take the gospel to the ends of the earth. This was a monumental responsibility. How would He choose from all of His followers? Again, prayer is the answer: "Now it came to pass in those days that He went out to the mountain to pray, and continued all night in prayer to God. And when it was day, He called His disciples" (Luke 6:12-13).

—The need to encourage and strengthen. A few days before choosing the Twelve, Jesus had given His first prophecy of the crucifixion and resurrection (Matthew 16:21). The disciples were confused. They wondered, "How could Jesus fulfill the prophecies of His coming kingdom if He were dead?" To answer their concerns, Jesus took three of His disciples to a mountain so they could be reassured of His coming kingdom. He wanted to give them a glimpse of the future and instill confidence in them. While on the mountain, Scripture says that "as He prayed, the appearance of His face was altered" (Luke 9:29). Prayer preceded what is referred to as "the transfiguration," and Jesus' change of appearance confirmed the future to Peter, James, and John.

—The completion of His ministry. Jesus knew what was coming. He knew His ministry on earth would soon end. And He also knew the implications for all mankind of His impending death. Yet the ending would still be extremely difficult. So Jesus prayed, "O My Father, if it is possible, let this cup pass from Me" (Matthew 26:39). But as He prayed a second and a third time, His prayer changed to one of strength of resolve: "O My Father, if this cup cannot pass away from Me unless I drink it, Your will be done" (verse 42).

A Lesson to Learn about Prayer

Scripture records Jesus praying before many of the important events and decisions in His life. Jesus began His ministry with prayer, and He ended His ministry with prayer. That should tell us something of the importance of seeking guidance and asking for strength through prayer. In His humanness Jesus chose to completely follow the Father in all things. When an important decision was to be made, Jesus went to the Father for wisdom and direction.

This should be your desire as well. What decisions must you make? What guidance do you need for the future? What strength is lacking for yourself and for others? Follow the Lord's example and, like Him, pray. God has given you a powerful resource in prayer. Don't fail to use its transforming and strengthening power.

Jesus was in the habit of praying—Jesus loved to pray. Prayer was a natural part of His life and was as important to Him as life itself. He not only prayed before important events and significant decisions, but He resorted to prayer in any and all other circumstances. Day and night, prayer was His way of life. Here are just a few of the many times Jesus prayed:

—Prayer in the midst of a busy life. Understandably, most people become stressed out or even give up in the midst of a crowded and busy schedule. But not Jesus. He had another way of dealing with the pressure of one hectic day after another. "In the morning, having risen a long while before daylight, He went out and departed to a solitary place; and there He prayed" (Mark 1:35).

—Prayer as an escape from popularity. You and I should never avoid an opportunity to model Christ before a watching world. But we also should never seek popularity or a position of power for the wrong reasons. Being in the public eye can lead to self-honor and pride. Jesus saw the danger of allowing Himself to become a popular idol. He obviously had no desire for this kind of fame. Observe how Jesus handled this: "Great multitudes came together to hear, and to be healed by Him of their infirmities. So He Himself often withdrew into the wilderness and prayed" (Luke 5:15-16).

—Prayer after success. After the return of a group of selected followers from a time of successful and fruitful ministry, Jesus prayed. He gave thanks to the Father for using the humble to make the ministry possible: "In that hour Jesus rejoiced in the Spirit and said, 'I thank You, Father, Lord of heaven and earth, that You have hidden these things from the wise and prudent and revealed them to babes'" (Luke 10:21).

—Prayer at a grave. Jesus' good friend Lazarus was dead. Jesus was about to preform a miracle of resurrection on His friend's body. In His heart He knew what was about to happen, but for the benefit of others, He "lifted up His eyes and said, 'Father, I thank You that You have heard Me...but because of the people who are standing by I said this, that they may believe that You sent Me'" (John 11:41-42).

—Prayer for the faith of a friend. Jesus tried to warn Peter of an upcoming test of his faith. Peter, however, was not yet aware of what was about to happen. Because of His concern for Peter's faith and His knowledge of the rigors of spiritual testing, Jesus said to Peter, "I have prayed for you, that your faith should not fail; and when you have returned to Me, strengthen your brethren" (Luke 22:32).

—Prayer for His enemies. How are Christians supposed to handle those who mistreat them? Who abuse them? Who unjustly accuse them? Who lie about them? Who cause pain in their lives? Jesus experienced all of these horrible situations, and He knew the perfect way to handle them. He prayed. He practiced what He preached in Luke 6:27-28: "I say to you who hear: Love your enemies, do good to those who hate you, bless those who curse you, and pray for those who spitefully use you." Even from the cross Jesus prayed, "Father, forgive them, for they do not know what they do" (Luke 23:34).

—Prayer from the cross. From the beginning to the end of His time on earth, Jesus modeled a life of prayer. In fact, His closing breath was used to pray, "Father, into Your hands I commit My spirit" (Luke 23:46). May we imitate Jesus' remarkable life of prayer at all times, including when we face our end.

A Lesson to Learn about Prayer

You cannot read very far in the Gospels without sensing the importance of prayer in the life of Jesus. He never failed to consult the Father before beginning His day.

And He never failed to thank the Father at the end of the day. The lesson is clear: If prayer was that important in the life of God the Son, shouldn't it be important to you and me as well? Why not affirm how important prayer is by nurturing the habit of prayer? "Rejoice always, pray without ceasing, in everything give thanks" (1 Thessalonians 5:16-18).

Jesus taught about prayer with fasting—Fasting was frequently practiced in connection with major events in the Bible. For example God's people fasted before confessing their sins (1 Samuel 7:6-10). Daniel fasted before he prayed to God about the restoration of the Jews to their homeland (Daniel 9:3). Paul and his team of missionaries prayed and fasted before making important decisions.

And we also see fasting in the life of Jesus. He fasted for 40 days after He was baptized (Luke 4:2). He taught about prayer and fasting (Luke 5:35). On one occasion He emphasized the need for prayer and fasting for a difficult issue (Matthew 17:21). He also assumed that fasting would be a normal part of a person's spiritual life when He said, "When you fast..." (Matthew 6:16).

A Lesson to Learn about Prayer

Fasting is not a common practice for most believers today. But throughout the centuries, Christians have benefited from the discipline of fasting as they focused on spiritual matters and on seeking God's wisdom on important issues. Jesus did not necessarily stress fasting, but He also did not discount it. He Himself fasted when He prayed. So the next time you have a serious decision to make or an urgent need for God's strength and wisdom, try fasting as you spend time in prayer.

Jesus taught others how to pray—Have you ever felt like you don't really know how to pray? You go to a prayer meeting and everyone there seems to be so natural and at ease as they pray. Afterward, when you walk away, you find yourself wishing someone could teach you how to pray.

That's what happened with Jesus' disciples. Many of them had watched John the Baptist pray. Then, as they followed Jesus, they watched Him pray. They saw His love for prayer, and as they listened to Him pray, they realized the power and benefits of prayer. So they came to the Master of prayer, and asked Him to teach them how to pray (Luke 11:1).

It was at this point in Jesus' ministry that He gave a model prayer—not only to His disciples then, but also to you and me, His disciples today. This prayer, found in Matthew 6:9-13, is what many refer to as "the Lord's Prayer." But, in reality, it is "the Disciples' Prayer." Jesus teaches us to pray "in this manner":

- Pray because of a relationship—"Our Father"

- Pray with respect and honor—"hallowed be Your name"

- Pray with an expectant heart—"Your kingdom come"

- Pray with a servant attitude—"Your will be done on earth as it is in heaven"

- Pray with dependence—"give us this day our daily bread"

- Pray as a sinner—"and forgive our debts"

- Pray with a forgiving heart—"as we forgive our debtors"

- Pray to have a discerning spirit—"and do not lead us into temptation, but deliver us from the evil one"

- Pray with an confident heart—"for Yours is the kingdom and the power and the glory forever"

A Lesson to Learn about Prayer

Jesus taught His followers how to pray by giving them a model prayer. He was not suggesting that this prayer, when prayed, is a special formula that ensures God will hear you. Rather, Jesus was merely giving a guide, a method, a sample of some of the elements that should be considered when you pray. This prayer in Matthew 6:9-13 is not meant to be merely memorized and recited with little or no thought. Words spoken in prayer have no meaning unless they are uttered from a sincere heart. So take the time to analyze the way you pray, and follow Jesus' model.

Jesus prayed for others—Intercession for others has been a dominant feature in the prayers we've looked at in this book. But with the prayers of Jesus in general, and His prayer in John 17 in particular, we see intercession taken to a new and celestial level. In John 17, Jesus prayed for His disciples then, and for us now, in what one has labeled the "Holy of Holies in the New Testament."[42]

This prayer, uttered just hours before Jesus' betrayal, trial, and crucifixion, is truly "the Lord's Prayer." Although it was prayed on earth, it reveals the Lord's future heavenly ministry of intercession. In this great prayer of communion of the Son with the Father, Jesus intercedes on three levels.

—First, Jesus prayed for Himself (John 17:1-6). He didn't pray for His rescue. Instead, He prayed that His obedience would lead Him back to the Father, back to the glory He had before His incarnation. He prayed, "I have glorified You on the earth. I have finished the work which You have given Me to do" (verse 4).

—Second, Jesus prayed for His disciples (17:6-19). He prayed that the Father would "keep them from the evil one" (verse 15) and "sanctify them" by the truth of God's Word (verse 17).

—Third, Jesus prayed for all believers (17:20-26). He looked down the corridor of time and prayed for all who would become believers. He prayed for their unity (verse 21), for the indwelling of the Spirit (verse 22), and that one day all believers would be with Him in heaven (verse 24).

A Lesson to Learn about Prayer

The world is a spiritual battleground. From Jesus' prayer in John 17 we learn that Satan and his forces are in a great struggle against God for the hearts and souls of men. Jesus, therefore, interceded and continues to intercede, asking the Father to keep you and me safe from Satan's power. Jesus prayed that the Father would keep us set apart, pure, and united under the banner of the truth of Scripture.

Are you following Jesus' example and praying for others? For their protection from the evil one? For their holiness? Are you praying for unity in your church and among believers? Knowing that Jesus is interceding for you and me should give us great confidence as we also pray and work for His kingdom.

Jesus prayed for prayer assistance—With the coming of Jesus and the cross, a new dimension was added to prayer. We in the New Testament age have Jesus praying for us (Hebrews 7:25). And, to further assist us, Jesus prayed to the Father to "give you another Helper, that He may abide with you forever" (John 14:16). That Helper is the Holy Spirit, who is an intercessor who prays with and for us, even when we don't know how to pray (Romans 8:27).

A Lesson to Learn about Prayer

What a resource you have in the Holy Spirit as a New Testament believer! Jesus promised not only to mediate for you at the right hand of the Father, but He has also given you a personal intercessor in the Holy Spirit. How mighty your prayers are as they ascend to God the Father, enriched by the ministry of God the Holy Spirit and mingled with the interceding prayers of God the Son.

With this amount of divine assistance, "far be it" that we would not be regularly involved in intercession (1 Samuel 12:23)!

Jesus was the greatest teacher who ever lived. His words instruct us today, and His example guides us. He taught the Twelve, and all believers since, how to pray by being a Man of prayer Himself. Like the disciples, who upon seeing their Master pray wanted to know how to pray, we too should want to learn how to pray.

If you want to know about the importance of prayer and how to pray, then read and study the prayers of Jesus. Witness His life of prayer for yourself. Make the accounts of His life and prayers your constant reading companion.

Prayer Principles for You—Diligence in Prayer

Prayer requires faith.

Prayer and faith are bound together. Faith is the inspiration for prayer, and prayer is the expression of that faith. Therefore, faith is fundamental to a successful prayer life. That's what Jesus meant when He said, "Whatever things you ask in prayer, *believing*, you will receive" (Matthew 21:22).

Prayer requires forgiveness.

Forgiveness is also required for a meaningful prayer life. The forgiveness of your sins through the finished work of Christ makes a right and open relationship with the Father possible. This undeserved forgiveness should prompt you to forgive others. Jesus taught that without a forgiving spirit, your prayers are meaningless. He instructed, "whenever you stand praying, if you have anything against anyone, forgive him, that your Father in heaven may also forgive you" (Mark 11:25).

Prayer requires sincerity.

Jesus declared that a person is to come to the Father in spirit and truth (John 4:24). He reacted to the insincerity of the prayers of the religious leaders of His day. He called His followers to refuse to pray for public approval or with a lack of sincerity. He said, "When you pray, you shall not be like the hypocrites. For they love to pray standing in the synagogues and on the corners of the streets, that they may be seen by men" (Matthew 6:5). The proper way to pray is with a sense of urgency and eagerness, realizing that you are approaching God Himself in prayer. When you have a heart heavy with burdens that need to be lifted, make sure you approach God with humble sincerity.

Prayer is to be a way of life.

Prayer should be as vital to you as eating, sleeping, and breathing. Your prayer life is not to be reserved for a certain day of the week or confined to a part of a religious ceremony. Prayer is a conversation with God, not with men, and belongs at the center of your ongoing relationship with God. The depth of Jesus' relationship with the Father was revealed by the amount of time He spent in prayer. When you pray, you reflect Jesus' very manner of life—a life of prayer.

A Prayer for Deligence in Prayer

Our Father, who art in heaven: Your Son Jesus, who is of Your very essence, knew it was vital for Him to stay in constant communion with You through prayer. May I recognize that as well; may I always possess a desire to lift up my voice to You in prayer. Stir within me an increased passion for prayer—I want to pray more often, and I want to pray more like Your Son prayed—constantly and fervently. Help me to pray boldly, believing that as I ask anything in Your Son's name, it will be given, for You have said that You hear and answer our prayers. Amen.[43]

Master List of Prayer Principles

Principles for Faith

Prayer guards you against taking matters into your own hands.

When you must make a decision, pray and ask, "What does *God* want me to do?" This shows your dependence on the Lord for His help and guidance.

Prayer guards you against making quick decisions.

If a quick decision is needed and there's no time to pray about it, the answer must be no. Make this a personal principle: "No decision made without prayer."

Prayer guards you against being influenced by family and friends.

Family and friends can be helpful, but when you pray, you are able to seek the infinite wisdom of God rather than the finite knowledge of man.

Prayer guards you against the influence of your culture.

Refrain from looking at your decisions-to-be-made through culturally colored glasses. Prayer forces you to ask, "God, what is Your standard?"

Prayer guards you against missing God's will.

To ensure that your feelings and desires don't hinder you from choosing God's will, pray until your heart and emotions are neutral and truly open to God's leading.

Principles for Humility

Prayer reviews your motives.

To do things God's way, you must put everything on pause to pray and appraise your motives by asking God, "Why am I doing this?"

Prayer refines your methods.

When you pray, "Lord, how would You have me do this?" God leads you into His will and shows you the methods to use or the way you should go.

Prayer restrains your emotions.

Avoid the consequences of emotion-based decisions by praying to God to quiet your heart. Remember, the wise person prays and obeys, while the fool sins and suffers.

Prayer revisits your options.

Talking through issues and alternatives with God allows you time to think and make the decisions that honor Him.

Prayer regulates your timing.

Your service to God is regulated by God's perfect schedule. Prayer helps you adjust your timing to God's plan and matures you while you wait.

Prayer recounts your resources.

When things look hopeless, coming to the Lord in prayer helps you remember God has already given you everything that pertains to life and godliness (2 Peter 1:3).

Principles for Gratitude

Prayer requires no manner or method.
Whether spoken or unspoken, prayer is the heart's earnest desire. Manner and method don't matter. What does matter is that you pray.

Prayer revives your joy.
Although praying may not change your circumstances, it allows you to experience joy in the midst of them. Turning your problems over to God enables you to face life's difficulties with joy.

Prayer restores your trust.
You can walk away from earnest prayer with complete trust that God has heard you and that your situation is in His hands. He will work it out (Romans 8:28).

Prayer releases your problems to God.
When nothing seems to be going right, and you feel barren and fruitless, pray. Through prayer you release your problems to the "great problem solver."

Prayer results in peace of mind.
God wants us to yield our anxieties to Him, and in exchange, He promises to give us inner peace.

Principles for Faithfulness

Prayer is a spiritual exercise for all ages.
No matter how young or old you are or what you do or don't know about prayer, you can pray. Simply talk to God. Prayer is a spiritual exercise anyone can participate in.

Prayer changes things.
The more you pray, the more you demonstrate your dependence upon God, and the more you will be transformed. Prayer makes you desire to live according to God's standards.

Prayer requires a pure heart.
Effective prayer calls for a pure heart. Follow the Bible's advice and examine yourself regularly. Ask God to search your heart, and make it a point to confess any and all your sins.

Prayer is the privilege of all believers.
No one understands how prayer works into the plans of a sovereign God. Yet God asks us to pray. Take this privilege seriously and determine to pray faithfully for others.

Prayer is the responsibility of all believers.
With every privilege comes responsibility. Scripture calls you to accept your obligation to pray without ceasing. Answer God's call to pray, and reap the blessings of a life of prayer.

Principles for Trust

Prayer gives you the right perspective.
It's easy to be distracted by the things of this world and lose sight of the bigger picture. Prayer helps you see things from an unlimited heavenly perspective.

Prayer should permeate your day.
Allow prayer to invade each hour and action of your day. Every breath taken in should become a prayer breathed out.

Prayer exhibits an attitude of trust.
When you pray, you are trusting God for His outcome. You are displaying an attitude of total trust in God's oversight of your life.

Prayer should be simple.
The most impressive prayers are those which are expressed with sincerity and simplicity. When you pray from your heart, your prayers will be simple and passionate.

Principles for Purpose

Prayer can be offered up anywhere and at any time.
God is everywhere all the time, so you can pray anywhere at any time. Never wait for the "right time" or "right place" to lift your prayers to our ever-present God.

Prayer is to be a constant habit and attitude.
An attitude of awareness of God leads to perpetual prayer. When God is always on your mind, prayer will become a habit, a way of life.

Prayer is not a substitute for action.
There is a balance we must seek between praying and acting, between faith in God and following God, between praying for God's will and doing God's will. Don't put off, in the name of prayer, doing an action that you know is right.

Prayer reveals your relationship with God.
Casual prayer never creates a close relationship with God. The amount of time you spend praying reveals the measure of your closeness to the Father.

Principles for Character

Prayer helps you better understand the mind of God.
While you might not see or understand the reasons for life's problems, through prayer, you can get a better grasp of God's will and intentions for you.

Prayer stimulates self-examination.
Through prayer, search for God's higher purpose in the twists and turns in your life. Thank Him, too, that His grace will sustain you through any and all of life's uncertainties.

Prayer refocuses your perspective.
When you find yourself focusing on your problems, pray instead and focus on the person of God. Prayer shifts your gaze away from yourself and upward to the throne of God.

Prayer restores relationships.
You cannot be angry at someone and, at the same time, pray for him or her. Prayer for those who have wronged or injured you aids forgiveness and restores relationships.

Principles for Determination

Prayer is your response to God's working.
God is constantly at work in history and in the lives of those around you. Your spiritual response is to partner with God and pray for others.

Prayer strengthens your relationship with God.
To nurture any relationship requires time. To better know God and to deepen your relationship with Him, commit to spending more time in prayer.

Prayer does not guarantee a positive answer.
The act of prayer does not guarantee you will get what you are praying for. Pray faithfully, and leave the answers to God.

Prayer allows you to reveal your deepest thoughts.
When you come into God's presence through prayer, freely expose your life to Him. Be honest, express your feelings, and open yourself up to His love.

Prayer fosters spiritual revival.
The common denominator in spiritual reawakening is prayer. When it comes to your own heart's fervor, prayer opens your soul to the Spirit's transforming power.

Prayer strengthens your determination.
It's easy to become discouraged. Prayer helps encourage us as we come to see our problems from God's perspective, and remember that nothing is too hard to Him.

Principles for Integrity

Prayer results in inspired vision.
A lack of prayer diminishes spiritual insight and leads to discouragement and defeat. Prayer reactivates spiritual vision and enables us to see through new eyes—God's eyes.

Prayer secures an instant audience with God.
You never need to ask for an audience with God. When you pray, you are instantly in the presence of the God of the universe.

Prayer results in inspired wisdom.
As you commune with God through prayer and study His Word, you receive the wisdom required to understand the things of God.

Prayer provides the necessary strength.
When you need spiritual energy, wait on the Lord in prayer. God will replace your weariness with His strength, and you will "mount up with wings like eagles" (Isaiah 40:31).

Prayer drives away fear.
There is no better way to grow in faith and trust in God than to be steadfast in prayer. Praying for courage and confidence transforms fear into faith.

Principles for Worship

Prayer prepares the way to accept God's will.
Life is a continuous uncut ribbon, a constant opportunity to choose to follow God. Praying regularly puts you in the habit of accepting God's will each day and each step of the way.

Prayer cultivates a heart of obedience.
Coming before God with the attitude of a submissive servant cultivates a heart that pleases God. You glorify Him when you pray to line up your will with His.

Prayer is an opportunity to praise and worship.
When you pray, you enjoy opportunity after opportunity to worship God and praise Him for His goodness and mercy. Magnify the Lord, and let your praise and worship flow.

Prayer is a reflective exercise.
Prayer is a discipline that requires thoughtful preparation. It requires that you reflect carefully on who it is you are addressing—God—and what you are requesting, and why.

Prayer generates spiritual strength.
It's a mystery, but prayer somehow strengthens, refreshes, and rejuvenates your soul. Talking things over with God reminds you that He is with you, even in the midst of pain and sorrow.

Principles for Passion

Prayer is to be with understanding.
Study God's Word and the prayers contained in it to learn how to pray with better understanding. Knowing more about God will enhance your conversations with Him.

Prayer is assisted by the Holy Spirit.
The Holy Spirit is a vital member of your prayer team. When you are not sure of what to say or how to pray, the Spirit will help you.

Prayer is to focus on spiritual concerns.
Focus your prayers on the spiritual realm. Physical needs have a place in intercession, but are secondary to praying for the spiritual welfare of others.

Prayer is not always answered immediately.
God's answers to your prayers may take years to come, but trust God for His timing and purpose for the answers. They will come at the right moment, when needed the most.

Principles for Diligence in Prayer

Prayer requires faith.
Faith is fundamental to a successful prayer life. Prayer and faith are bound together. Faith is the inspiration for prayer, and prayer is the expression of that faith.

Prayer requires forgiveness.
Forgiveness is required for a meaningful prayer life. The forgiveness of your sins through Jesus Christ makes it possible for you to pray and leads you to forgive others.

Prayer requires sincerity.
Jesus taught that a basic element of prayer is to exhibit respectful sincerity, and realize you are approaching God Himself. When you come to Him, come with a humble spirit.

Prayer is to be a way of life.
Prayer should be as vital to you as eating, sleeping, and breathing. It belongs at the center of your ongoing relationship with God and should be a way of life.

Notes

1. See Genesis 17:1-6.

2. Herbert Lockyer, *All the Prayers of the Bible* (Grand Rapids: Zondervan, 1973), p. 31.

3. See Deuteronomy 32:3-4; Psalm 61:2; 1 Peter 2:6.

4. Fred H. Wight, *Manners and Customs of Bible Lands* (Chicago: Moody Press, 1978), p. 136.

5. As cited in Terry W. Glaspey, *Pathway to the Heart of God* (Eugene, OR: Harvest House Publishers, 1998), p. 76.

6. J.C. Ryle, as cited in Terry W. Glaspey, *Pathway to the Heart of God* (Eugene, OR: Harvest House Publishers, 1998), p. 24.

7. See 1 Samuel 1:3,11,24.

8. As cited in Paul L. Tan, *Encyclopedia of 7700 Illustrations* (Rockville, MD: Assurance Publishers, 1984), p. 1052.

9. See Colossians 1:9; 1 Thessalonians 5:25; 2 Thessalonians 3:1.

10. See 1 Samuel 3:9; 15,22; Psalm 40:8.

11. 1 Samuel; 2 Samuel; 1 Chronicles 11–29.

12. Charles Caldwell Ryrie, *The Ryrie Study Bible* (Chicago: Moody Press, 1976), p. 436.

13. J.D. Douglas, ed., *The New Bible Dictionary* (Grand Rapids: Eerdmans Publishing Co., 1978), p. 1322.

14. Psalm 139:1-2; 140:1; 141:1.

15. See Psalm 23:1,4.

16. Rick Warren, *The Purpose-Driven Life* (Grand Rapids: Zondervan, 2002), p. 17.

17. Warren, *The Purpose-Driven Life,* p. 17.

18. The Hebrew calendar dates are Kislev to Nisan, 1:1–2:1.

19. Nehemiah 2:19; 4:1-3; 4:7-23; 6:1-4; 6:5-9; 6:10-14; 6:17-19.

20. See also Nehemiah 4:9; 6:9,14.

21. See also verses 19, 25, 27, and 32.

22. Lockyer, *All the Prayers of the Bible,* p. 95.

23. See Nehemiah 13:22,31.

24. See Job 19:25.

25. Joni Eareckson, *Joni* (Grand Rapids: Zondervan, 1977).

26. Lockyer, *All the Prayers of the Bible*, p. 138.

27. See Jeremiah 11:18-23; 26:15-16.

28. See Jeremiah 7:16; 11:14; 14:11.

29. Robert Jamieson, A.R. Fausset, David Brown, *Commentary on the Whole Bible* (Grand Rapids: Zondervan, 1971), p. 611.

30. See Jeremiah 11:19-21; 12:6; 20:1-2; 20:10; 26:8; 36:23.

31. See Jeremiah 32:17; Lamentations 3:21-23.

32. See Ezra 8:23; Nehemiah 9:1; Esther 4:1,3,16.

33. See Daniel 9:3.

34. William Hendricksen, *Exposition of the Gospel According to Luke* (Grand Rapids: Baker Books, 1978), p. 110.

35. See Luke 1:46-55.

36. E.M. Bounds, *The Complete Works of E.M. Bounds on Prayer* (Grand Rapids: Baker Books, 1990), p. 544.

37. See 1 Samuel 1:7,18; 7:6; Nehemiah 1:4; Daniel 9:3; Luke 4:2.

38. John MacArthur, Jr., *1 & 2 Thessalonians* (Chicago: Moody Press, 2002), p. 186.

39. See Prison Epistles: Ephesians, Philippians, Colossians, Philemon.

40. See Romans 1:9; Ephesians 1:16; Colossians 1:9; 1 Thessalonians 1:2.

41. See Romans 1:1; Ephesians 1:3; Revelation 4:11.

42. Lockyer, *All the Prayers of the Bible,* p. 227.

43. See Matthew 6:9.

Personal Notes

Personal Notes

Personal Notes

Personal Notes

_____

_____

_____

_____

_____

_____

_____

_____

_____

_____

_____

_____

_____

_____

_____

_____

_____

_____

_____

Personal Notes

Other Books by Jim George

A Man After God's Own Heart

Many Christian men want to be men after God's own heart...but how do they do this? George shows that a heartfelt desire to practice God's priorities is all that's needed. God's grace does the rest.

A Man After God's Own Heart Devotional

This book is filled with quick, focused devotions that will encourage your spiritual growth, equip you to persevere when life gets tough, manage your responsibilities well with wisdom, and live with maximum impact in all you do.

A Husband After God's Own Heart

You'll find your marriage growing richer and deeper as you pursue God and discover 12 areas in which you can make a real difference in your relationship with your wife.

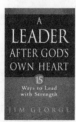

A Leader After God's Own Heart

Every man is either a leader or a leader in the making—whether at work, in the home, or any other setting. So what does it take to be a good leader—one God can use? This book will equip you to lead with strength and have a positive, lasting impact.

The Man Who Makes a Difference

How can you have a lasting impact? Here are the secrets to having a positive and meaningful influence in the lives of everyone you meet, including your wife and children.

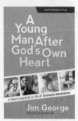

A Young Man After God's Own Heart

Pursuing God really *is* an adventure—a lot like climbing a mountain. There are many challenges on the way up, but the great view at the top is well worth the trip. This book helps young men to experience the thrill of knowing real success in life—the kind that counts with God.

A Young Man's Guide to Making Right Choices

This book will help teen guys to think carefully about their decisions, assuring they gain the skills needed to face life's challenges.

A Young Man's Guide to Discovering His Bible

This book will help teen guys make the Bible their personal guide in all they do. They'll learn many great tips for exploring God's Word and getting the most out of it.

The Bare Bones Bible® Handbook

The perfect resource for a fast and friendly overview of every book of the Bible. Excellent for anyone who wants to know the Bible better and get more from their interaction with God's Word.

The Bare Bones Bible® Handbook for Teens

Based on the bestselling *Bare Bones Bible® Handbook*, this edition includes content and life applications specially written with teens in mind. They will be amazed at how much the Bible has to say about the things that matter most to them.

10 Minutes to Knowing the Men and Women of the Bible

The lessons you can learn from the outstanding men and women of the Bible are powerfully relevant for today. As you review their lives, you'll discover special qualities worth emulating and life lessons for everyday living.

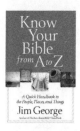

Know Your Bible from A to Z

This is a concise, easy-to-understand A-to-Z survey of the Bible's most important people, places, customs, and events. A great help for understanding the big picture of the Bible and applying the Scriptures to your daily life.

A Boy After God's Own Heart

This book helps boys learn how to make good decisions and great friends, see the benefits of homework and chores, get along better with their parents and siblings, and get into the Bible and grow closer to God.

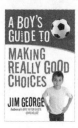

A Boy's Guide to Making Really Good Choices

Making good choices is the biggest step a boy can take toward growing up. This book helps boys learn to make the best kinds of choices—those that make them stronger, wiser, and more mature.

God Loves His Precious Children
(coauthored with Elizabeth George)

Jim and Elizabeth George share the comfort and assurance of Psalm 23 with young children. Engaging watercolor scenes by artist Judy Luenebrink and delightful rhymes by Jim and Elizabeth bring the truths of each verse to life.

God's Wisdom for Little Boys
(coauthored with Elizabeth George)

The wonderful teachings of Proverbs come to life for boys. Memorable rhymes play alongside colorful paintings for a charming presentation of truths to live by.

An Invitation to Write

Jim George is a teacher and speaker and the author of several books, including *A Man After God's Own Heart*. If you would like to receive more information about other books by Jim George, to sign up for his mailings, or share how *Knowing God Through Prayer* has influenced your life, you can contact to Jim at:

   goodreads

www.JimGeorge.com